PASTOR MRS. SHADE OLUKOYA

Violence

against

NEGATIVE
VOICES

THE BATTLE CRY CHRISTIAN MINISTRIES

VIOLENCE AGAINST NEGATIVE VOICES

OVERPOWERING THE NEGATIVE VOICES

Shade Olukoya

VIOLENCE AGAINST NEGATIVE VOICE
Shade Olukoya

Published 2009 AD
Re-printed - 2011 AD

ISBN 978-9783831889

CONTENTS

Chapter 1

THE VOICE
OF GOD

Of all voices in the world, the voice of God stands. Interestingly, there are over seven billion voices all over the world. These billions of voices often come out with individual and unique differences for each speaker. In actual fact, no voice is insignificant. Even the voice of a child is as important as the voice of an adult. The Bible tells us that, all the voices in the world have their values or their importance.

> There are, it may be, so many
> kinds of voices in the world, and
> none of them is without
> signification. **1 Cor. 14:10.**

DISTINCT VOICES

Here the Bible recognises the fact that even though there is a cacophony of voices from pockets of people all over the world, yet the voices convey messages that cannot be ignored. What the Bible tells us is this, since there are many nations, communities, people and groups, each segment of the society has a peculiar voice or language. Each of these voices have its distinct articulation, pronunciation, emphasis and localised meanings. Hence, nobody should joke with the significance of voices.

No wonder, a lot of destinies and lives have been influenced by voices. We cannot do without voices neither can we ignore voices. The only thing we can do is to bar the influence of negative voices and embrace the positive influence of godly voices.

TYPES OF VOICES

Here we discover that there are three types of voice;

1. The voice of God.
2. The voice of the enemy, the devil.
3. The voice of man.

The only voice that is completely positive and beneficial is the voice of God. The voice of the enemy; on the other hand, is filled with hatred, wickedness and negative influences. The voice of man is mostly negative. Although a few times, men and women can be influenced and inspired to speak kind, positive, beneficial, edifying and words that build up.

A FRESH UNDERSTANDING

It has come to a point in the world where we need to come up with a fresh understanding of the fact that our destiny rises or falls on the kinds of voices which we imbibe. Listening to negative voices all the time, will build up a negative atmosphere. Listening to positive voices, will induce a positive mental attitude.

MOTIVATIONAL TALKS

The trend in the world today, is to make people listen to motivational speakers. The reason for this is that, it has become a common knowledge that the society will become a better place when positive motivational and inspirational words are listened to time and again. The only missing ingredient in these motivation talks is solid scriptural contents. No matter the inspirational words men and women hear, once it lacks scriptural or heavenly contents, there is a limit to what people can benefit from such talks or speeches.

Consider the kind of voice you will like to hear, when you have lost a father, a mother or an uncle. What type of voice will you like to hear when you are in the throes of discouragement? Can you describe the content of words you will like to listen to when you are going through a trauma? Wouldn't you rather love to listen to words that will calm down your anxious nerves, comfort you and give you hope in a hopeless situation?

This explains why one word from God is greater than a thousand voices. When God speaks, all earthly voices will fade into insignificance. When God speaks, the voice of man will be forgotten. When God utters one word, a million words spoken by man would be rendered null and void.

SIMPLY INCOMPARABLE

There is a world of difference from the different voices of man and the unique voice of the Almighty. God's voice is incomparable, His words are unchallengeable and what He utters has the capacity to shut the mouth of lions, gag the mouth of your enemies and render their spoken words to become inconsequential.

When you are sick and tired of hearing the voice of man, you need to tune to the frequency of heaven and hear the Almighty clearly. When human voices have brought you tears, you need a word from God to wipe the tears away. When human voices have dribbled you to a point of confusion, you need the voice of the Almighty to place you on the right track.

The voice of God is the only voice you can hear and never miss your step. The voice of God is the only voice you can listen to and you will never get derailed.

When human beings speak of hopelessness, a word from God will give you hope. When human beings speak words of condemnation, the word of God will bring justification. When human beings are trying to fill your ears with negative words, that can urge you to contemplate suicide, God's word will remind you of the fact that it is not all over. When words that are negative tend to tell you that all hope is lost, words of assurance will flood your heart and God will tell you that yours is a hope that is glorious beyond comparison.

ONE WORD FROM GOD

When all you hear are words that have built an evil stronghold in the garden of your heart, one word from God will dismantle the stronghold and build a structure of uncommon blessing, which will take your destiny to a level of unprecedented favour.

The voice of God is so strong, that it will penetrate fortified structures erected by the enemy. Then you will be able to get God's best. The voice of God will also make you to become who and what God wants you to be.

What does it take to hear the voice of God? We need a fresh understanding of the power that resides in the voice of God. This understanding will arm us with what it takes to benefit from the voice of God and thereby overcome all negative voices. The results will be wonderful.

Since the beginning of the creation of man, and throughout all generations, God has portrayed His voice as one unique voice that can never be ignored by man. The voice of God has brought out prisoners from the dungeons of affliction, saved souls gloriously, transformed destinies uniquely and brought breathtaking changes to the lives of men and women.

The book of job tells urges us to pay attention to the voice of God, which is loud enough to arrest our attention, capture our interest and make us to hear the voice of God.

> *Hear attentively the noise of his voice, and the sound that goeth out of his mouth. He directeth it under the whole heaven, and his lightning unto the ends of the earth. After it a voice roareth: he thundereth with the voice of his excellency; and he will not stay them when his voice is heard.*

God thundereth marvellously with his voice; great things doeth he, which we cannot comprehend.
Job 37:2-5

IT IS AWESOME

The sound that goes out of God's mouth is as awesome as His power, as glorious as His attributes and as compelling as His majesty. God's word can never be ignored. God's voice sounds like a mighty roar. It blasts through the entire universe like a thunder.

Whenever God speaks, he loads His words with power, decks it with honour and dignity and garnishes it with flavours that will keep you asking for more. If you find yourself in a trackless desert, the word of God will bring you out. The word of God will bring you out of the deepest dungeon and catapult you to great heights.

When God speaks, all other voices will become silent. When God speaks, the enemy is disgraced. When God speaks, evil voices are silenced. When God speaks, evil verdicts are revoked. When God speaks, every accusation from the kingdom of the enemy will be rendered null and void. When God speaks, the whole earth will keep silent. God's voice is the voice of an internal decree which no one can challenge or nullify.

PLEASANT PLACES

The voice of God, is the only voice you need to settle your case and validate your divine claims. Let the voice of God be spoken on your behalf today and your case will be taken from the realm of darkness to the courts of the God, who rules in heaven and on earth.

The moment God's word sounds on your behalf, all your enemies will be sentenced to confusion, shame and failure. When God puts in a word for you, you will experience victory in the human court and things will fall into pleasant places.

> *The LORD is the portion of mine inheritance and of my cup: thou maintainest my lot. The lines are fallen unto me in pleasant places; yea, I have a goodly heritage.*
> ***Psalm 16:5-6***

NOTES:

Chapter 2

THE SCHOOL OF HEARING THE DIVINE VOICE

One amazing fact about God's voice is that there is no other voice like it. When God speaks to His children, He makes use of the still-small voice. The voice could be a whisper, an inner nudge and a silent assurance but it will be so compelling that you will know that it is the voice of God. The scriptures below reveal the characteristics of God's words when they are targeted towards His children.

> And thine ears shall hear a word behind thee, saying, this is the way, walk ye in it, when ye turn to the right hand, and when ye turn to the left. **Isaiah 30:21**
>
> And he said, Go forth, and stand upon the mount before the LORD. And, behold, the LORD passed by, and a great and strong wind rent the mountains, and brake in pieces the rocks before the LORD; but the LORD was not in the wind: and after the wind an earthquake; but the LORD was not in the earthquake: And after the earthquake a fire; but the LORD was not in the fire: and after the fire a still small voice. And it was so, when Elijah heard it, that he

> *wrapped his face in his mantle, and went out, and stood in the entering in of the cave. And, behold, there came a voice unto him, and said, what doest thou here, Elijah?* **1 Kgs 19:11-13**

A GENTLE VOICE

God either speaks with the still small voice or He makes you to hear a gentle voice telling you that it is well with you. When God speaks to His children, He speaks with tenderness and assurance. But it is quite different when His voice sounds against the kingdom of darkness or against your enemies.

> *Hast thou an arm like God? Or canst thou thunder with a voice like him?* **Job 40:9**

THE SOUND THUNDER

The Bible tells us that God thunders out with His voice. The sound of God is the sound of thunder. The voice of God is the voice of warfare. When He speaks, He sends war signals to the camp of the enemy The voice of God is not gentle at all, when it comes to dealing with the enemy.

The LORD also thundered in the heavens, and the Highest gave his voice; hail stones and coals of fire. Yea, he sent out his arrows, and scattered them; and he shot out lightnings, and discomfited them.
Psalm 18:13-14

When God wants to fight, He makes use of terrible weapons. His voice takes up the sound of thunder, accompanied by hailstones and coals of fire. Moreover, lightening is an instrument of warfare in the hands of God. The voice of the Almighty is threatening in the ears of satanic agents. His voice can become so acidic that, it can melt anything that stands like a barrier.

The heathen raged, the kingdoms were moved: he uttered his voice, the earth melted. **Psalm 46:6**

When God utters His voice, the whole earth can melt like a wax. This shows us that, the voice of God is mighty. When God sends out His voice, it comes out in a mighty form. It is my prayer, that God will send out His voice and the might of His voice, will send a cold chill down the spines of your stubborn pursuers.

To him that rideth upon the heavens of heavens, which were of old; lo,

*he doth send out his voice, and that
a mighty voice.* **Psalm 68:33**

THE SCHOOL OF DIVINE VOICE

The Bible has told us quite a lot about the voice of God. The Psalmist having attended the school of power, discovered quite a lot about, the voice of the Lord. He devoted a whole Psalm to a wonderful exposition on the voice of God.

What believers lack today, is a clear understanding of the characteristics, the properties and the distinctiveness of the voice of the Almighty. God's voice is so unique, that it is loaded with solutions to every problem man would ever have. It has power. To unleash terror on the enemy's camp and give you victory. The passage below speaks volumes about the voice of the Lord.

> *The voice of the LORD is upon the waters: the God of glory thundereth: the LORD is upon many waters. The voice of the LORD is powerful; the voice of the LORD is full of majesty: The voice of the LORD breaketh the cedars; yea, the LORD breaketh the*

cedars of Lebanon. He maketh them also to skip like a Calf; Lebanon and Sirion like a young unicorn. The voice of the LORD divideth the flames of fire. The voice of the LORD shaketh the wilderness; the LORD shaketh the wilderness of Kadesh. The voice of the LORD maketh the hinds to calve, and discovereth the forests: and in his temple doth every one speak of his glory **Psalm 29:3-9**

From this passage, you will discover that the voice of the Lord can be heard everywhere. The busy traveler can hear the voice of God; the skilful craftsman can perceive God speaking to him in clear terms. The lonely housewife can listen to the tender loving voice of God. The discouraged can hear the voice of encouragement coming from the throne of the Almighty. The confused can hear the voice of God pointing the way out of chaos into an unmistakable direction.

The voice of God can calm anxious nerves and rock you to sleep, when you are bothered by troubles within and without. The voice of God can give hope to the hopeless, help to the helpless, strength to the weary and power to those who are faint hearted.

NOTES:

_____

_____

_____

_____

_____

_____

_____

_____

_____

_____

_____

_____

_____

_____

_____

_____

_____

_____

_____

_____

Chapter 3

THE TRANSFORMING POWER OF GOD'S VOICE

The voice of God can come with transforming power, to change the unchangeable, love the unlovable and reform those who have been given up by all. The voice of the Almighty can speak to you, even when it appears that you are lost in the crowd.

The voice of God can lift you up, from the lowest dungeon and move you with the force of power to the mountain top of promotion, peace, settlement and power.

The voice of God can penetrate thick darkness and envelope you with dazzling light. The voice of God can provoke divine rainfall upon you and satiate the weary soul. The voice of God can open closed doors, break down barriers and break asunder the gates of brass. The voice of God can thunder and frighten your enemies until they confess that you are too hot to handle.

The voice of God can revoke the handwriting of darkness, cancel the verdict of wickedness and render null and void, every decree promulgated by your enemy, The voice of God, can be enveloped by fire and consume every cobweb of darkness. The voice of God can take you from the point where you are and place you at the place where God wants you to be.

THE VOICE OF POWER

The voice of God can heal the broken hearted, calm your troubled waters and give you peace like a river. The voice of God is powerful enough, to make the enemy tremble and flee. The voice of God can make the thief of your destiny to surrender what he has stolen.

The voice of God can provoke the enemy to begin a journey of self destruction. The voice of God can make the enemy to hear a sound which no one else will hear. Such a sound, will either frighten the enemy to drop the spoils of war or surrender; saying that your singular voice have been converted to the voice of thousands of people coming up with an invasion against their camp.

SENT ON A PANIC FLIGHT

No matter how strong the cedars of Lebanon are, the voice of the Lord can break them asunder. The voice of God can send your enemies on a panic flight. They will begin to run helter-skelter under hot pursuit. The voice of God will cause such a panic that the enemy will go into fits of madness. The voice of the Lord is so strong that, it can divide the flames of fire.

> *The voice of the LORD*
> *divideth the flames of fire.*
> ***Psalm** 29:7*

There is no place on earth where the voice of God cannot be heard. The voice of God can distort the voice of the enemy and make those who have been sent to attack you to hear counter instructions and begin to work against themselves. The voice of God can be heard either in the palace or in the forest. The voice of God can be heard by the high and the mighty and they will be compelled to carry out divine instructions.

The voice of God is so unique that no one can imagine the extent the voice of the Almighty would go. The voice of God can protect every department of your life. The voice of God can serve as an alarm, when anyone wants to tamper with your destiny. The voice of God can be so recorded powerfully that it will scream, "Touch not my anointed", whenever anyone dares you or your God.

The voice of God has been so strongly built that, it will prevent thieves, invaders, attackers and archers from meddling with your destiny. The voice of God has been charged with authority to make you pursue your pursuers, destroy your destroyers, attack your attackers and kill those who have been mandated `to kill you.

LOADED WITH THUNDER

The voice of the Almighty is loaded with thunder, hailstones, lightening, fire, arrows of deliverance and every weapon which the Almighty has manufactured, in order to disgrace the enemies of your destiny. The moment you understand the uniqueness of the voice of God and the limitless abilities embedded in it, you will be imbued with uncommon boldness, divine strength and the type of power that cannot be insulted.

The voice of God carries the anointing of God. The voice of God carries the authority of God. The voice of God is a symbol of the awesome power of the Almighty. The voice of God has creative abilities. The voice of God is a powerful war machine. The voice of God is stronger than the deadliest nuclear warhead in the world.

The voice of God portrays the totality of the height, the length and the breadth. Yes, the entire gamut of the power of the Most High God. It is true that the voice of God is a carrier of the totality of the power of God. The voice of God tells a lot about the magnitude of the power of God. Let us examine the following characteristics of the voice of God.

1. **The voice of God is unique**: There is no voice on earth like God's voice. No voice can be compared with the voice of God. The sound of the voice of God comes in a unique manner. When you listen to all kinds of voices and the voice of God comes up, you will know that you are listening to a voice that is so special that it cannot be measured by any yardstick for measuring human voices.

   Since you were born, you have listened to several voices. But the only voice that has come to you in a unique manner is the voice of the Creator of heaven and earth. Tell me, which voice can be so unique as to bring something out of nothing, and order out of chaos, except the voice of God.

   At the beginning of creation, God simply spoke the world into existence. Immediately God declared, "Let there be", there was. The world of nature and all creatures, including human beings were brought into existence through the instrumentality of the voice of the Almighty.

   And the earth was without form,
   and void; and darkness was upon

the face of the deep. And the Spirit of God moved upon the face of the waters. And God said, Let there be light: and there was light. And God saw the light, that it was good: and God divided the light from the darkness. And God called the light Day; and the darkness he called Night. And the evening and the morning were the first day And God said, Let there be a firmament in the midst of` the waters, and let it divide the waters from the waters. And God made the firmament, and divided the waters which were under the firmament from the waters which were above the firmament: and it was so. **Genesis 1:2-7**

And God said, Let there be lights in the firmament of the heaven to divide the day from the night; and let them be for signs, and for seasons, and for days, and years: And let them be for lights in the firmament of` the heaven to give

light upon the earth: and it was so. And God made two great lights; the greater light to rule the day, and the lesser light to rule the night: he made the stars also. And God set them in the firmament of the heaven to give light upon the earth, and to rule over the day and over the night, and to divide the light from the darkness: and God saw that it was good. And the evening and the morning were the fourth day. And God said, Let the waters bring forth abundantly the moving creature that hath life, and fowl that may fly above the earth in the open firmament of heaven.
Genesis 1:14-20

Only a unique voice, could have brought the work of creation into reality. No doubt, the voices of satanic agents are capable of perpetuating destruction. But they lack the ability to create good things. Only the voice of God, can make things to happen even when there has been nothing in existence. This unique voice is at your disposal as you tarry in the place of prayer, you can be privileged to hear a unique voice that will change confusion to perfect order, sadness to happiness and lack to plenty.

The unique voice of the Almighty will sound to your advantage and your life will no longer be the same again. Even those who have vowed that as long as they are alive, you will not amount to anything, will be forced to rise up and favour you after listening to the unique voice of the Almighty. You can pray and ask God to manifest His unique voice in your present circumstances. At the end of the day your story will change, your sorrow will cease, your tragedy will stop and your failure will be turned to success. Amen!

2. **The voice of God is the voice of power**: One of the key characteristics of God is that, it is so loaded with power that no power on earth can challenge it. When the voice of power sounds out, lesser powers will take a bow. When powers of darkness come up with an evil programme, thinking that they will succeed because they have a measure of power, they will be disgraced. There is a principle in the spiritual realm and it goes thus; when a greater power and a lesser power go into a contest, the lesser power will be defeated. Hence, when the voice of power

sounds out, other voices of lesser or elemental powers must, of necessity, take a bow. When they take a bow it is a symbol of their total defeat. The enemy cannot have a last laugh against you. The enemy cannot prevail as long as the voice of power is speaking victory on your behalf. All you need to do is to move into a realm where the voice of power is speaking good things concerning your life. The; voice of power will automatically grant you victory in the battlefield of life. God does not have to go anywhere in search of power. Power is resident in Him.

The Bible says;

> God hath spoken once; twice have
> I heard this; that power belongeth
> unto God. **Ps. 62:11**

Power is the exclusive preserve of the Almighty. Power begins and ends with God. So even when God speaks once, the fact that power belongs unto God will be relayed universally even with double emphasis. The voice of power is the voice you need today. With the voice of power entering into your spirit man, weakness will disappear and divine strength will take over.

NOTES:

_____

_____

_____

_____

_____

_____

_____

_____

_____

_____

_____

_____

_____

_____

_____

_____

_____

_____

_____

_____

_____

Chapter 4
THE VOICE OF AUTHORITY

The voice of God is the voice of authority. God's voice is loaded with authority. Authority portrays the fact that there is nothing on earth that God cannot do. There is no sphere of human experience where the authority of the Almighty cannot be displayed. When the voice of authority sounds against the marine kingdom, marine powers will bow. The authority that resides in the voice of the Almighty is so strong that would control the world of nature. The voice of authority was demonstrated by Jesus in *Mark 4:35-41*

And the same day, when the even was come, he saith unto them, Let us pass over unto the other side. And when they had sent away the multitude, they took him even as he was in the ship. And there were also with him other little ships. And there arose a great storm of wind, and the waves beat into the ship, so that it was now full. And he was in the hinder part of the ship, asleep on a pillow: and they awake him, and say unto him, Master, carest thou not that we perish? And he arose, and rebuked the wind, and said unto the sea, Peace, be still. And the wind ceased, and there was a great calm. And he said unto them, why are ye so fearful? How is it that ye have no faith? And they feared exceedingly and said one to another; what manner of man is this, that even the wind and the sea obey him? **Mark 4:35-41**

INCOMPARABLE POWER

The world of nature was on a riot. The Bible teaches us that there arose a great storm of wind. The storm was so violent that water gushed into the ship. The rush of the water was threatening. Ordinarily the sea or the storm has no master. No earthly voice can order a storm to be calm.

There is nothing in science or nature that can really stop a violent storm. Once the storm starts, no command or authority can stop it. But during the earthly ministry of the Lord Jesus Christ, He proved that the voice of God is a voice of authority. While the disciples were thrown into a panic, Jesus was asleep like a baby: While the disciples were frightened stiff, Jesus even had pillow in the midst of the storm.

What else but authority could have given a man such an unshakable confidence and uncommon peace?

The ship of those days was not as comfortable as our modern ship. For someone to use a pillow shows that the person has uncommon authority. The disciples shouted; "Carest not thou that we perish". It took time before they could realise that the use of the pillow was a symbol of authority. The words of the disciples and the word of Jesus was different. They spoke with fear but Jesus spoke with authority; hence, His words were few; "Peace, be still".

Jesus knew that everything in this world, including the voices of nature recognises greater authority since they have ears. They can hear when a higher power issues a command. Jesus knew the kind of authority He had at His command. Immediately He pronounced; "Peace be still" the wind ceased and there was a great calm. He had to challenge them saying; "why are you so fearful?" The disciples were so amazed that they had to say; "what manner of man is this?" In other words they were saying; "What manner of authority is this?"

The authority that makes a storm to stop suddenly is no mean authority. When God bestows His authority upon you through the influence of His spoken words, you will experience supernatural dominion.

UNCOMMON AUTHORITY

Wherever you go, you will find an avenue for demonstrating uncommon authority which issues from the Almighty. Not only is the voice of God able to demonstrate authority over the world of nature, it is also able to demonstrate authority over evil spirits. The story of the mad man of Gadara bears an eloquent testimony to the fact that absolute authority issues from the Almighty.

> And they came over unto the other side of the sea, into the country of the Gadarenes. And when he was come out of the ship, immediately there met him out of the tombs a man with an unclean spirit, who had his dwelling among the tombs; and no man could bind him, no, not with chains: Because that he had been often bound with fetters and chains, and the chains had been plucked asunder by him, and the fetters broken in pieces: neither could any man tame him.

And always, night and day, he was in the mountains, and in the tombs, crying, and cutting himself with stones. But when he saw Jesus afar off, he ran and worshipped him, And cried with a loud voice, and said, what have I to do with thee, Jesus, thou Son of the most high God? I adjure thee by God, that thou torment me not. For he said unto him, Come out of the man, thou unclean spirit. And he asked him, What is thy name? And he answered, saying, My name is Legion: for we are many And he besought him much that he would not send them away out of the country. Now there was there nigh unto the mountains a great herd of swine feeding. And all the devils besought him, saying, Send us into the swine, that we may enter into them. And forthwith Jesus gave them leave. And the unclean spirits went out, and entered into the swine: and the herd ran violently down a steep place into the sea, (they were about two thousand;) and were choked in the sea. And they that fed the swine fled, and told it in the city and in the country. And they went out to se what it was that was done. And they come to Jesus, and see him that was possessed with the devil, and had the legion, sitting, and clothed, and in his right mind: and they were afraid. And they that saw it told them how it befell to him that was possessed with the devil, and also concerning the swine. And they began to pray him to depart out of their coasts. And when he was come into the ship, he that had been possessed with the devil prayed him that he might be with him. Howbeit Jesus suffered him not, but saith unto him, Go home to thy friends, and tell them how great things the Lord hath done for thee, and hath had compassion on thee. And he departed, and began to publish in Decapolis how great things Jesus

> had done for him: and all men did
> marvel. **Mark 5:1-20**

If there is any incident in the ministry of the Lord Jesus Christ that validates the fact that the voice of God is the voice of authority, it is this story. Here was a man have been beaten black and blue by wicked demons. They had targeted this man as the man to bastardise and destroy completely Note the fact that the day his mother gave birth to him, he came out as a normal child. No demonic arrows, no spell of insanity and no attack on his brain.

ARROW OF INSANITY

One day the man became a victim of the arrow of insanity; insanity of the highest dimension. The demons banished him from civilised society. Perhaps, if he had been a mere mad man on the streets, he would have had access to leftover food and occasional gifts from those who may decide to toss coins or food items out of pity. His own insanity took him to the graveyard. When the Bible says no man could bind him, not even with chains, it shows that efforts were probably made to bind him.

Read verse four again.

> *Because that he had been often bound with fetters and chains, and the chains had been plucked asunder by him, and the fetters broken in pieces: neither could any man tame him.* **Mark 5:4**

The powers that inhabited him were so violent that even when fetters and chains were used to bind him, he tore them like a piece of weak thread. Everyone who tried to tame him were stupefied by the fact that he had gone beyond the stage where he could be tamed. It was a pathetic situation. What the man suffered are painted graphically to make us realise the fact that demons have a measure of wicked authority.

> *And always, night and day he was in the mountains, and in the tombs, crying, and cutting himself with stones.* **Mark 5:5**

He moved between the graveyard and the mountains nearby; perpetuating a mission of self destruction. The man was crying when no one was beating him and he was busy cutting himself with sharp stones. That kind of existence can be likened to being dead while one is alive. The attack on him tells us of the extent the devil can go to destroy human lives. When the enemy goes on rampage, nobody can determine the extent of damage and destruction that will be perpetuated.

While there was terrible inner turmoil. There was a terrible riot within. For a man to cry while cutting himself at the same time portrays a high degree of insanity. The man was so insane that mad people would call him mad.

In the society we have degrees of madness. Among the Yoruba community, some people are called mad people who put on clothes (Were Alaso) This term is used to describe people who appear so gentlemanly that there would be no inclination whatsoever that they are suffering from madness. Some people come up with fits of madness occasionally. They can spend nine months of the year portraying sanity while for the next three months; it will be madness on parade.

For such people, the degree of madness may appear mild but the man described in the fifth chapter of the book of Mark is a victim of acute madness. He was so mad that he could inflict a terrible injury upon himself. Regardless of the pain of the injury he kept on inflicting more painful injuries. This shows that the devil is "wickedly wicked and badly bad! ·

NOTES:

_____

_____

_____

_____

_____

_____

_____

_____

_____

_____

_____

_____

_____

_____

_____

_____

_____

_____

_____

_____

Chapter 5

THE ENEMY'S WICKEDNESS

Whenthe enemy wants to attack, he throws pity to the dustbin. The case of this man shows us that, wickedness is the devils stock-in-trade. It takes a kind of supernatural power to break chains and fetters. Victims of madness often demonstrate such extraordinary powers. They are known to have cut fetters and chains to pieces. Such victims may go without food for days on end, yet their strength will remain unabated.

Tell me, is there any power that can control such people? If a man has broken all chains and cut asunder all fetters and if such a man could not be tamed by anyone, what type of authority will make him to surrender? It is the authority of the Almighty. This is an authority that has no equal. God is the number one authority in heaven and on earth according to the scriptures.

Primarily; He rules in heaven.

> _And all the inhabitants of the earth are reputed as nothing: and he doeth according to his will in the army of heaven, and among the inhabitants of the earth: and none can stay his hand, or say unto him, What doest thou?_ **Dan. 4:35**

God has absolute authority in heaven and on earth. So, what happened when the mad man who could not be tamed it caught a glimpse of Jesus

> *But when he saw Jesus afar off,*
> *he ran and worshipped him,*
> **Mark 5:6**

MATCHLESS AUTHORITY

Jesus exudes uncommon authority. Just the sight of Him invoked compelling worship from the madman, he ran as if he was pursued by some powers to acknowledge the authority of Jesus. He did it through worship. Think about this; how could a mad man who paid no attention to any instruction given by man, who ignored every attempt to make him calm down a bit and fought defiantly against every effort to stop him from inflicting wounds upon himself become normal?, Yet without any chain, any fetter, any tranquilizer or any antipsychotic drug to induce sanity. The man changed gears and began to worship Jesus. What a matchless authority!

The next thing he did was to cry with a loud voice.

> *And cried with a loud voice, and*
> *said, What have I to do with thee,*
> *Jesus, thou Son of the most high*

*God? I adjure thee by God, that thou torment me not. **Mark 5:7***

THE MOST SUPREME AUTHORITY

What the mad man said depicts the fact that he recognised the authority of Jesus Christ as the most supreme authority on earth. The mad man could not employ the use of any other authority except the authority of the Most High God when he said; "I adjure thee by God that thou torment me not". As soon as the mad man was done with acknowledging the authority of Jesus, a word of command came from the lips of Jesus.

To understand the fact that the voice of God is the voice of authority, you need to pay a close attention to the reply of the mad man of Gadara. The onlookers must have wondered why such a madman could worship Jesus: They must have also wondered why the man was sane enough to hold a meaningful conversation with Jesus Christ.

Why Jesus said "What is your name; the commanding demon gave out its name as legion. The man was just a single soul but the resident demons were many Unknown to those who have tried to tame the mad man, there was a whole garrison of demonic spirits trading and living in the man.

A LEGION

The devil is so wicked that he had to put a legion in the life of one mad man. When the chief demon said that its name was legion, he quickly added that they adopted that name because they were many. A good understanding of the military formation at the time of Jesus will help us in this direction.

The name legion was given to a division in the Roman army. It did not always denote the same number; but, in the time of Christ, it consisted of six thousand- three thousand foot and three thousand horsemen. It came, therefore, to signify a large number, without specifying the exact amount.

A WICKED INVASION

The human mind, can not fathom the implication of such an invasion. The mad man of Gadara had in him enough demons to destroy a city. When the demons were cast out, they were more than enough to enter over two thousand pigs. This shows that some demons would have had no place to enter as the pigs were not enough.

God has given us the ministry of deliverance and it is indeed a strange ministry. Many people do not know the impact of what God had used us to do. The ministry of deliverance is a wonderful ministry. Who would have thought that this notorious madman had thousands of demons living in him? They had converted the man to a mobile house.

Thank God for the authority of Jesus. Just one word, thousands of demons were evicted. As God has given us the ministry of deliverance, we keep giving God the glory for the voice of authority. It takes this kind of voice to send demons packing and make the captives to become free.

DEMONS MUST OBEY

The authority, which Jesus demonstrated, has remained a matchless authority. He has shown us that, He is the only one who can speak to demons and they have no choice but to obey: He is the only one who can order evil spirits and they have no option than to obey every order given to them.

The beauty of this story is that, demons had to beg Jesus to allow them to go into the swine. The demons knew that they entered into the mad man by making use of a level of authority but the beauty of the power of the Most High God is as we say in Nigerian English; "Power pass power". The demons could not even go into the swine without recognising the authority of Jesus. Beloved, the story is not yet complete. As soon as the evil demons came out of the mad man. He became a complete gentleman.

> *And they come to Jesus, and see him that was possessed with the devil, and had the legion, sitting, and clothed, and in his right mind: and they were afraid.* **Mark 5:15**

A man who could not put on normal clothes had to be given a dress which he wore and he sat down calm, cool and collected. The Bible tells us that he was in his right mind. The man was so transformed that he requested for permission from Jesus to be with Him. But Jesus simply told him to take up the mission of an evangelist who would proclaim the message of salvation to friends and family members.

A GREAT WITNESS

The man became a great witness to the power and authority of God, which is able to save to the uttermost simply because the voice of authority freed him from the shackles of madness. A man who once inflicted brutal wounds on himself became as gentle as a dove simply because the authority of the God of heaven and earth made lesser authorities to bow.

My prayer is that the authority of heaven will speak one word into your life and your destiny will become a specimen of what the voice of authority can accomplish even when the enemy has made desperate efforts cage you. Whatever evil authorities have declared. God has declared that every counsel of darkness shall fail. Since the Bible has declared;

There are many devices in a man's heart; nevertheless the counsel of the LORD, that - shall stand. *Prov. 19:21*

No authority in heaven and on earth can match the authority that comes from God. Embrace the voice of power today and your life will never be the same again.

NOTES:

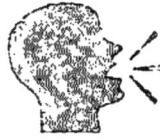

Chapter 6

VICTORY
IS
SURE

In this chapter we shall explore an uncommon portrait of the divine voice. The voice of God rings out with a tone of finality. When God speaks, it is the end of discussion. Let us examine two special attributes.

1. **The voice of finality**: We hear voices all the time. It is quite common for human beings to draw conclusions or make comments that borders on some forms of finality. When it appears that a voice has made a final comment, God will rise with the real voice of finality and order fake voices to be swallowed up. It is easy for men and women to use their mouth to proclaim that all hope is lost and there is nothing anyone can do any longer. But the truth is that only God has the final say. When human beings and enemies speak and declare that a full stop has been put in place, God will prove them wrong and convert their evil full stop to a comma. From that moment, then final full stop of the Almighty will be put in place and God will put a seal of finality as what God has declared will become final.

> *God forbid: yea, let God be true,*
> *but every man a liar; as it is written,*
> *that thou mightest be justified in*

thy sayings, and mightest overcome when thou art judged.
Rom. 3:4

It is indeed very interesting, for you to sit by and watch people declare severally what they adjudged to be their own kind of finality, only for God to come on the scene and erase the final verdicts of men and women and put His own imprint of unchallengeable finality. When you know that the voice of God is the voice of finality, people's comment and statement or even what may pass for their temporary verdicts will not move you. Since you know that when the Ancient of Days speaks, His voice rings with notes of finality.

2. **The Voice of victory:** The world is a battlefield. On daily basis, we grapple with battles of various dimensions. There is no day without its battle. There is no destiny that is battle free. A life that is without battles can only be found in the graveyard, but as long as you are alive, you will experience all kinds of battles. But the good news is that, we need not be frightened by the fact that fighting battles is a common experience as far as mankind is concerned.

> *Many are the afflictions of the righteous: but the LORD delivereth him out of them all.* **Ps. 34:19**

The Bible has not told us that the righteous will be without afflictions. Afflictions will definitely be many but the Bible has given us one glorious assurance that, the Lord will deliver us from every one of them. God has not promised us life without problems. Problems may come but what we need is victory

Again, the Bible tells us;

> *So shall they fear the name of the LORD from the west, and his glory from the rising of the sun. When the enemy shall come in like a flood, the Spirit of the LORD shall lift up a standard against him.* **Isa. 59:19**

Here the Bible highlights one undeniable fact; the enemy can come like a flood. In other words there can be a deluge of attacks but the more the attacks are, the more glorious our victory shall be. The enemy may threaten you with the voice of battle but the Bible makes it very clear that God has vowed that He will always rise up a standard against the wicked machinations of the enemy

The sound of war may sound repeatedly but God has decided that He will raise His standards because of you. There is a mystery behind the phrase "raise the standard". The person who raises the standard determines the victory

THE WINNER

Let me explain what I mean. In a football match, the goal is to score. No matter how good the players are, no one can relish sweet victory until goals are scored. Can you imagine a football tournament whereby the referee decides that the goal post will be shifted. At that point, it is only the referee that can determine when goals are scored.

Now; you can picture a game between you and the forces of darkness. The force of the enemy makes frantic efforts to score several goals. As they are about to score, God in heaven mandates an angel to shift the goal post to your favour. The captain of the enemy fires a long shot but by the time it reaches the goal post, the goal post has been shifted and there is no goal. If the football tournament continues like that, the enemy will end in frustration because no one is sure where the goal post will be positioned next.

When the enemy fires a shot, it can be likened to the enemy coming in like a flood. But before the flood will enter into the boat of your life, God would have raised a new standard; a standard that will dribble and confuse the enemy. God will never allow them score a single goal, as the mystery of the shift of goal posts will work to your favour. When it gets to a point, those who belong to the camp of the enemy will become so confused that they will begin to score what is regarded as own goals. This is made very clear in the scriptures.

> *And I will feed them that oppress thee with their own flesh; and they shall be drunken with their own blood, as with sweet wine: and all flesh shall know that I the LORD am thy Saviour and thy Redeemer, the mighty One of Jacob.* **Isa. 49:26**

At that point, the enemy will be fed with his own flesh and be made to be drunk with their own blood. There is nothing as wonderful as to send the enemy on a mission of self destruction.

> *And he shall snatch on the right hand, and be hungry; and he shall*

*eat on the left hand, and they shall not be satisfied: they shall eat every man the flesh of his own arm: **Isaiah 9:20***

The voice of victory is wonderful. When you take the battle to the gates of the enemy and the voice of victory sounds on your behalf, whatever has been done to oppress you, will be swallowed up by your victory as one voice from God will validate your victory and settle the fact that you have won. The voice of victory is all you need to prove to the world that the battle will always be on the side of the one who comes up with victory May God speak the voice of victory and may all your battles become converted to testimonies in Jesus name. Amen!

NOTES:

_____

_____

_____

_____

_____

_____

_____

_____

_____

_____

_____

_____

_____

_____

_____

_____

_____

_____

_____

_____

_____

_____

_____

Chapter 7
THE HOLY HARMONIOUS VOICE

There is nothing as glorious as being settled by the voice of peace and harmony when you are threatened by a chastic situation

The voice of God is the voice of peace. Peace is a very scarce commodity in a world that is ravaged by hostility, anxiety, problems and multiple attacks from the kingdom of darkness. People go from the north to the south in search for peace. A lot of people have struggled with problems such that they have not been given a moment's rest. There are people who go about with wars within and without.

> *For, when we were come in to Macedonia, our flesh had no rest, but we were troubled on every side; without were fighting's, within were fears.* **2 Cor. 7:5**

The above passage gives us a very graphic picture of practical situations in life. Most of the time, we are pressed beyond measure. We are bombarded by problems from every direction. When there are multiple attacks, problems of all shapes and sizes, inner turmoil, external aggression and all kinds of problems, what is needed is peace. We need the voice of peace to speak against the backdrop of rumours of war, wars, satanic gang ups, evil reports and all forms of situations that come up suddenly to cause confusion in the lives of God's children.

A GREAT CALM

When the voice of peace is spoken by God Almighty, there would be a great calm. Many people approach the upsurge of crises, the multiplication of problems and all forms of satanic complications with panic but all we need to do is to hear the voice of peace once and the God who makes wars to cease will come on the scene and change the situation.

> *He maketh wars to cease unto the end of the earth; he breaketh the bow; and cutteth the spear in sunder; he burneth the chariot in the fire. Be still, and know that I am God: I will be exalted among the heathen, I will be exalted in the earth. The LORD of hosts is with us; the God of Jacob is our refuge. Selah.* **Ps. 46:9-11**

No matter the intensity of the war which you are going through, God is able to make a change. The Bible refers to Him as the God of peace in the passages below

Now the God of peace be with you all. Amen. **Rom. 15:33**

Those things, which ye have both learned, and received, and heard, and seen in me, do: and the God of peace shall be with you. **Phil. 4:9**

And the very God of peace sanctify you wholly; and I pray God your whole spirit and soul and body be preserved blameless unto the coming of our Lord Jesus. **1 Thess. 5:23**

Now the God of peace, that brought again from the dead our Lord Jesus, that great shepherd of the sheep, through the blood of the everlasting covenant, **Heb. 13:20**

And the God of peace shall bruise Satan under your feet shortly. The grace of our Lord Jesus Christ be with you. Amen. **Rom. 16:20**

HEAVENLY TRANQUILITY

When God refers to himself as the God of peace, it shows that His presence in your life will envelop you with peace. What type of peace are we talking about? It is the peace of God which passes all understanding.

> *And the peace of God, which passeth all understanding, shall keep your hearts and minds through Christ Jesus.* **Phil. 4:7**

When the Bible says that the peace of God passes all understanding, it simply means that it is a kind of peace that is simply incomprehensible. This kind of peace comes up when someone has been bombarded by problems, bad news, evil threats, harassment by debtors, hostile conditions, evil reminders by satanic emissaries and thoughts that remind you of past failures and crises.

But you suddenly hear the voice of peace and all problems disappear in a twinkle of an eye simply because, the voice of the Almighty has dissolved every negative situation.

This kind of peace truly passes all understanding. You will not be able to explain what has just happened. Those who are around you will begin to wonder if you are human at all. They will begin to pinch themselves to be sure that you are not a ghost. That they are not dreaming. Of course, that is what happens when the God of peace steps into your affairs and every form of agitation, unrest, deep-seated fear, demonic anxiety, repeated palpitations of the heart and every crisis sponsored by the kingdom of darkness will give way

Interestingly, Jesus is the Prince of peace. The sound of His voice drives away every unrest. His appearance in your circumstances puts a break on every vehicle of problems that are sponsored by satanic agents. When the voice of peace sounds from the throne of grace, peace will swallow chaos, there will be heavenly tranquility.

NOTES:

Chapter 8

THE VOICE OF GOD IS THE VOICE OF WISDOM

The voice of God is the voice of wisdom. Then God utters His voice, it is loaded with is uncommon wisdom. The wisdom we are referring to here, differs significantly from worldly wisdom. There are three types of wisdom.

1. The wisdom of man
2. The wisdom of the devil
3. The wisdom of God

The Bible has drawn a line of demarcation between heavenly wisdom and earthly wisdom.

> *Who is a wise man and endued with knowledge among you? Let him shew out of a good conversation his works with meekness of wisdom. But if ye have bitter envying and strife in your hearts, glory not, and lie not against the truth. This wisdom descendeth not from above, but is earthly, sensual, and devilish. For where envying and strife is, there is confusion and every evil work. But the wisdom that is from above is first pure, then peaceable, gentle, and easy to be intreated, full of*

mercy and good fruits, without partiality, and without hypocrisy. And the fruit of righteousness is sown in peace of them that make peace. James 3:13-18

WISDOM FROM ABOVE

There is a wisdom that descends from above. There 'is a type of wisdom that is earthly. There is a type of wisdom that is sensual. There is also a type of wisdom that is devilish. The quality of wisdom is known by the fruits it produces. When wisdom gives birth to strive, confusion and every evil work, it shows that the origin of that type of wisdom is satanic.

A lot of voices which we hear are loaded with satanic wisdom. Such voices leave the hearers, sad, confused, hopeless and wrongly motivated. Whenever you hear certain voices and thoughts of suicide, apathy and rejection floods your heart, you are simply listening to the voice of the devil.

The devil specialises in speaking dark words. He takes the delight in speaking words that will lead you astray even when such words are couched with evil wisdom.

Nobody can say that the devil has no wisdom. It is through his evil wisdom that he is able to attack, deceive, and lead people astray. The Bible makes it very clear however that there is pure wisdom, this type of wisdom comes from above.

THE QUALITIES OF PURE WISDOM

The characteristics are listed below

1. **It is pure** - When you hear the voice of wisdom from God, it comes with purity. There is no guile in it. is so pure that there is no falsehood in it.

2. **It is peaceable** - In order words, it brings out the fruits of peace. When it is the voice of wisdom, the result will be peace; peace like a river will flood your soul.

3. **It is gentle** - it is the voice of wisdom from above; there will be no fear in it. It is so calm. Gentleness is one of the fruits of the spirit.

> *But the fruit of the Spirit is love, joy; peace, longsuffering, gentleness, goodness, faith,* ***Galatians 5:22***

The voice of wisdom, is the voice of gentleness. There is no harshness whatsoever in it. It is so gentle because it is the voice of wisdom. Paul the Apostle was divinely connected with the voice of wisdom. Hence, he manifested Christ like gentleness in order to show us what it takes to manifest gentleness.

> *Now I Paul myself beseech you by the meekness and gentleness of Christ, who in presence am base among you, but being absent am bold toward you:* ***2 Cor. 10:1***

4. **The voice of wisdom is easy to be entreated** - You do not have to coarse anybody to do what you like as wisdom flows naturally. It is when it is different from the voice of wisdom that people go into extraneous arguments; But when the voice of wisdom is at work, both the hearer and the listener will sail smoothly.

5. **The voice of wisdom is the voice of mercy** - Such a voice is so full of mercy that it will minister mercy to the hearers. God is the God of mercy. The wisdom that flows from Him will produce mercy. The type of mercy we are referring to is divine mercy hence, the term "full of mercy". When God utters the voice of wisdom, mercy will cascade from heaven like an avalanche.

O give thanks unto the LORD, for he is good: for his mercy endureth for ever. **Psalm 107:1**

O give thanks unto the LORD; for he is good: because his mercy endureth for ever. **Psalm 118:1**

Praise ye the LORD. O give thanks unto the LORD; for he is good: for his mercy endureth for ever. **Psalm106:1**

Let the house of Aaron now say; that his mercy endureth for ever: **Psalm 118:3**

When the Bible declares that God's mercy endures forever, it tells us that whenever we stand in need of the ever enduring mercy of God, we are sure He will be there for us.

As we go through this word, there will be instances of personal mistakes and there will be occasions when you can be victims of false accusation. Either it is for your own mistake, or for false accusations, you need God's mercy.

> *It is of the LORD'S mercies that we*
> *are not consumed, because his*
> *compassions fail not.*
> **Lamentations 3, 22**

The mercy of God is a product of His compassion. God is kind and compassionate. He is so full of mercy that His bowels of compassion will make Him to pity the fatherless, care for the needy and forgive the penitent.

6. **The voice of wisdom produces good fruits -** So much effort has been made to fully explore the qualities of the voice of God. When you hear God's voice, you will be amazed by the amount of good fruits it will produce. The voice of God is the voice of wisdom that produces abundant fruits. The more of God's voice you hear, the more your life will be filled with good fruits.

7. **The voice of wisdom is without partiality -** Since it is free from diplomacy and cunning wisdom, the voice of wisdom offers free and equal opportunities to all. Most of what people utter are often towards partiality. But the moment it is the voice of wisdom, impartiality and justice will be the characteristics.

8. **The voice of wisdom is without hypocrisy -**
    In the voice of wisdom, there will be nothing like
    hypocrisy whereas the wisdom of man will
    produce hypocrisy; God's wisdom will always be
    without any from of adulteration, double dealing
    and lying. We need more of the voice of wisdom
    in our life, if we must become instruments in the
    hands of God to change the world.

NOTES:

Chapter 9
THE VOICE OF COMFORT

The voice of God is the voice of comfort. The journey of life, may take us through different turns, corners, byways and tracks, the ups and downs of life might have taken its toll upon many lives. Many are hurting. Multitudes are bruised. A good number of men and women have been wounded by the jagged saw of adversity. Many are hurting simply because they have been maligned, castigated, accused wrongly and deceived by people whom they trusted. A lot of wives are victims of battery assault, misunderstanding and injustice. A lot of church members have been treated badly by fellow believers and friends.

TRAUMATIC EXPERIENCES

Many young converts have gone through traumatic experiences. The problem with the world today is that the percentage of those who carry ugly scares of hurt, pain, and offences is very high. Many people are crying saying "Is there no balm in Gilead" Hence, there is a great need for the ministry of comfort.

The ministry of comfort can only be received through the voice of comfort. God knows your pain. He knows what you have gone through. He knows what you have passed through even when no one seems to understand. Beloved, let me encourage you, God is not dispassionate.

The Bible says;

> *For we have not an high priest which cannot be touched with the feeling of our infirmities; but was in all points tempted like as we are, yet without sin.* **Hebrews 4:15**

Jesus is our high priest. He is always touched with the feelings of our infirmities. Therefore, He knows what you have gone through. He will reach out to you at the nick of time with the voice of comfort. God cannot leave His people without the voice of comfort. He cannot allow His people to remain in pain, sorrow and sadness without reaching out to them.

THE MINISTRY OF COMFORT

God has said it loud and clear that His people must be comforted, encouraged, motivated and made happy.

> *Comfort ye, comfort ye my people, saith your God.* **Isaiah 40:1**

> *Nevertheless God, that comforteth those that are cast down, comforted us by the coming of Titus;* **2 Cor. 7:6**

God is the one who comforts those who are cast down. Hence whenever we hear his voice, we are blessed with the ministry of comfort. No wonder, the Bible refers to the Holy Spirit as the comforter. We often hear of believers going about with depression simply because they have not been able to benefit meaningfully from the voice of comfort. No matter what you go through, the testimony of Paul the apostle will be yours, if you are a beneficiary of the ministry of comfort.

> *We are troubled on every side,*
> *yet not distressed; we are*
> *perplexed, but not in despair;*
> *Persecuted, but not forsaken;*
> *cast down, but not destroyed;*
> **2 Cor. 4:8-9**

DIVINE COMFORT

How can someone be troubled on every side and be not distressed? How can someone be perplexed and not be in despair? How can someone who is persecuted testify to the fact that he is not forsaken? How can someone get to a point when he or she is cast down and the person comes out victorious without being destroyed? It is simply because such a person has benefited from the voice of comfort.

The voice of comfort is a voice that comes from above. When all earthly voices fail to comfort you, the voice that comes from heaven, will comfort, strengthen and encourage you. Listen to the voice of comfort today and your life will never remain the same. The voice of God will establish you as you go through the pilgrimage of life. The voice of God will pour the oil of comfort on your troubled waters. The voice of comfort will do something new in your life.

1. **The voice of prophecy**: The voice of God is the voice of prophecy. When we journey through the wilderness of life, we need to hear from above. The voice of prophecy is the voice that sounds from heaven speaking with accuracy to the situations which we pass through. If we depend on our knowledge, our experiences and our wisdom, we will surely fail. But when we allow God to meet us at the point of our needs by giving us an accurate prescription through prophecy we will experience pleasant surprises.

The spirit of prophecy comes out with the voice of prophecy. One of the characteristics of the voice of prophecy is that it ushers testimonies into the lives of the hearers.

And I fell at his feet to worship him. And he said unto me, See thou do it not: I am thy fellow servant, and of thy brethren that have the testimony of Jesus: worship God: for the testimony of Jesus is the spirit of prophecy. *Revelation 19:10*

YOUR TESTIMONIES

Once you hear the voice of prophecy you will come up with testimonies that will glorify Jesus. What is prophecy? Prophecy is speaking forth the word of God concerning a particular future event. It is foretelling what will happen sooner or later. The voice of prophecy brings the future to the present through the spirit of God. Prophecy is foretelling what has not happened but will happen in the future.

Often times, we ignore the voice of prophecy which comes out when our fathers in the Lord speak to us the deep things in the mind of God. The moment the voice of prophecy is in place in your life, you will never lack divine direction.

PROPHETIC DIRECTIONS

The early Church experienced the voice of prophecy practically. God spoke to His people clearly, without hiding anything. Every step was taken by divine direction. For example when the early Church needed to take a step concerning global evangelization, the Lord spoke prophetically.

> *Now there were in the church that was at Antioch certain prophets and teachers; as Barnabas, and Simeon that was called Niger, and Lucius of Cyrene, and Manaen, which had been brought with Herod tetrarch, and Saul. As they ministered to the Lord, and fasted, the Holy Ghost said, Separate me Barnabas and Saul for the work where unto I have called them. And when they had fasted and prayed, and laid their hands on them, they sent them away. So they, being sent forth by the Holy Ghost, departed unto Seleucia; and from thence they sailed to Cyprus.* **Acts 13:1-4**

They were busy ministering to the Lord through fasting, when the Holy Ghost came with a powerful prophetic instruction. Thus, they were led by the voice of prophecy.

NOTES:

Chapter 10

THE VOICE OF TRUTH

We need the voice of truth. The voice of God is the voice of truth. We live in a world dominated by error and lying. The truth has become a scarce commodity. People now say what they never meant and they never declare what they mean.

Hence, what we have today is a situation where lying and falsehood have almost swallowed the truth. We have a precarious situation on our hands.

DISTORTION OF THE TRUTH

The world is filled with the following distortion of the truth.

1.   Diplomacy
2.   Outright lying.
3.   Half truth.
4.   Exaggeration.
5.   Silence when the truth should be told.
6.   False witness.
7.   Double talk or speaking from both sides of the mouth.
8.   Speaking copiously
9.   Swearing falsely in order to claim that one is telling the truth.
10. .Using words to confuse the people in order to avoid telling the truth.

11. Blowing little things out of proportion.
12. Non-verbal lying; making use of the face to conceal the truth.
13. Partial lie and partial truth.
14. Hypocrisy.
15. Selling lies to people in the name of truth.
16. Saying what one does not mean.

These and other manipulations of the truth are rife today but the Bible says;

> *Buy the truth, and sell it not; also wisdom, and instruction, and understanding* ***Prov. 23:23***

THE COST

The truth about the truth is that it is costly. No matter how costly the truth is, every effort must be made towards buying it. If you dwell on falsehood and lying, you will be ashamed when the truth comes out. The truth of the matter is that lie may travel a thousand miles but sooner or later the truth will catch up with it. Unfortunately; we have become so used to lying and telling the truth has become difficult. Thank God, God remained truth even when men have chosen to remain as liars.

The Bible says;

> *God forbid: yea, let God be true, but every man a liar; as it is written, That thou mightest be justified in thy sayings, and mightest overcome when thou art judged.* ***Rom. 5:4***

The Almighty is truth personified.

> *For true and righteous are his judgments: for he hath judged the great whore, which did corrupt the earth with her fornication, and hath avenged the blood of his servants at her hand.* ***Rev. 19:2***

TRUTH OR ERROR

The choice is yours, to either listen to the voice of falsehood or to the voice of truth. Remember, falsehood will always produce falsehood, while truth will always produce truth. You must saturate your spirit man by listening to the voice of truth.

Interestingly and yet unfortunately the world has been dominated by falsehood and lying. Over the airwaves, through the television and radio, through the telephone and via the print media, the world has remained soaked in lying. There is a lot of propaganda on the television and people are fed with political lies day in day out over the radio.

Users of mobile phones can lie that they are at their workplace while they are somewhere running evil errands for the devil. The GSM has made it possible for someone to be in western Nigeria and declare that he is at Abuja, the federal capital territory

PROMOTION OF LIES

The world has promoted lies and relegated truth to the background. Therefore, those who have decided to stand for the truth are despised simply because, the people of the world believe that you have to lie in order to prove that you are smart. We must shun the evil propaganda of the world and load our lives with the truth of the word of God.

SATURATION METHODS

You can saturate your life with the truth in the following ways.

1. Meditate on the scriptures.
2. Memories the scriptures
3. Listen to the word of God during Church services.

4. Saturate yourself with the truth by playing powerful audio/ video messages.
5. You can listen to the Bible in audio or video formats.
6. You can buy posters of scripture captions.
7. Rather than make use of ancient jokes and proverbs, quote the word of God copiously
8. Read live changing books.

Interestingly, Dr. Olukoya the general overseer of the M. F. M. ministries has authored hundreds of books on a wide array of subjects including spiritual warfare, deliverance, Christian worship, Christian service, Christian living, Christian motivation etc. You can read these books in order to listen to the voice of truth.

One area you cannot neglect; in order to load your spirit man with the truth is the area of prayer and spiritual warfare. To stem the tide of evil propaganda which can build fear into your heart, you need to pray.

VICTORY OVER FEAR

Fear, is one of the weapons of the kingdom of darkness used to make people believe a lie rather than the truth. The word fear can be spelt out in an acronym.

F - False
E - Evidence
A - Appearing
R - Real

If you want to deal with your fear you need to pack into your spirit man truths of the word of God. After you are done with programming the truth into your mind and your Spirit, you need spiritual warfare. Here, the G. O.'s best selling books come in handy

1. Prayer your way to breakthroughs
2. Prayer Ram
3. Prayer Passport

These prayer books contain tools for unprecedented victory in the school of solution warfare. When you pray aggressively error and falsehood will be flushed out and the voice of truth will have unfettered access to your destiny

More than anytime in the history of the world, we need the voice of truth today shun the voice of error and embrace the voice of truth coming from the throne of God.

NOTES:

_____

_____

_____

_____

_____

_____

_____

_____

_____

_____

_____

_____

_____

_____

_____

_____

_____

_____

_____

_____

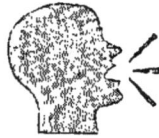

Chapter 11

THE VOICE
OF
ASSURANCE

Τ he voice of assurance is very scarce. The voice of doubt and despair abound. God has given us the voice of assurance to dispel discouragement. Meditate on the hymn below and you will get a feel of the power of the voice of assurance.

BLESSED ASSURANCE

1. Blessed assurance, Jesus is mine!
   O what a foretaste of glory divine!
   Heir of salvation, purchase of God,
   born of his Spirit, washed in his blood.

Chrs: *This is my story this is my song,*
   Praising my Saviour all the day long;
   This is my story this is my song,
   Praising my Saviour all the day long.

2. Perfect submission, perfect delight,
   visions of rapture now burst on my sight;
   angels descending, bring from above
   Echoes of mercy whispers of love.

3. Perfect submission, all is at rest;
   I in my Saviour am happy and blest,
   watching and waiting, looking above,
   filled with his goodness, lost in his love.

One of the greatest problems today can be traced to the fact that men and women lack assurance or confidence. Many are battling with inferiority complex, lack of assurance, timidity, fear of the unknown and fear of the future. Many do not know what the next minute may unfold, hence they live in fear. Many are afraid of bad news. Many fear to go to bed at night. Waking up to face a new day is also a problem to people.

WHEN WE NEED ASSURANCE

Assurance is needed to face the battles of life. Divine assurance is what we need to tackle the enemy. We need to be assured of victory even before the commencement of the battle. We need divine assurance when the enemy's threats continue to mount up. We need assurance in the face of depleting inner strength. We need assurance when we face hatred and criticism. We need assurance when friends become enemies. We need assurance when our confidants choose to tread the path of betrayal.

We need assurance of heaven when we are persecuted by family members, taunted by co-workers and despised by those to whom we turn to for help. We need assurance from the throne of mercy when our prayers seem to bounce back from the ceiling.

THE JOURNEY OF FAITH

We need assurance when we are undertaking the journey of faith. We need assurance when old problems continue to rear up their ugly heads. We need assurance when enemies gather like never before, to launch an attack against us. We need assurance when evil powers muster their efforts in order to strike. We need assurance when we are in the throes of disappointment or when we experience unfulfilled promises.

We need assurance, when human help prove inadequate. We need assurance when we encounter nagging health problems. We need assurance, when friends are distant and helpers are nowhere in sight. We need assurance, when winning and victory appear difficult.

MOMENTS OF TRIALS

We need assurance, when our problems try to make us doubt the ability of the Almighty. We need assurance, when we face isolation, segregation and rejection. We need assurance, when we do not know where the next meal will come from. We need assurance when there are not enough resources to tackle debts, challenges, obligations and commitments.

What a wonderful experience it is to say "Blessed assurance, Jesus is mine. Herein lies the mystery of life. Most of the time we know what we ought to do, most of the time we have the right ideas, most of the time we have taken the right decisions, but are just not sure if we are on the right track. Therefore, many have abandoned their dreams just when they are about achieving the unachievable or experiencing the unprecedented. At such a time all that such people need is the voice of assurance.

BLESSED ASSURANCE

Most times, many of us would have given up, thinking that we do not know what to do. But thank God for the voice of assurance. We have taken the right steps, followed the right path, executed the right ideas and achieved outstanding successes. If the voice of assurance is removed from the world, humanity would go the rampage. People will commit suicide as a result of depression and hopelessness. But the voice of assurance will always help when it appears that all hope has been lost.

ASSURANCE SCRIPTURES

Let me give you a few assurance scriptures to help you benefit maximally from the voice of assurance;

Fear thou not; for I am with thee: be not dismayed; for I am thy God: I will strengthen thee; yea, I will help thee; yea, I will uphold thee with the right hand of my righteousness. **Isa. 41:10**

For I the LORD thy God will hold thy right hand, saying unto thee, Fear not; I will help thee. **Isa. 41:13**

Fear not, thou worm Jacob, and ye men of Israel; I will help thee, saith the LORD, and thy redeemer, the Holy One of Israel. **Isa. 41:14**

The LORD is my shepherd; I shall not want. He maketh me to lie down in green pastures: he leadeth me beside the still waters. He restoreth my soul: he leadeth me in the paths of righteousness for his name's sake. Yea, though I walk through the valley of the shadow of death, I will fear no evil: for thou art with me; thy rod and thy staff they comfort me. Thou preparest a table before me in the presence of mine enemies: thou anointest my head with oil; my cup runneth over. Surely goodness and mercy shall follow me all the days of my life: and I will dwell in the house of the LORD for ever. **Psalm 23:16**

I the LORD have called thee in righteousness, and will hold thine hand, and will keep thee, and give thee for a covenant of the people, for a light of the Gentiles; **Isa. 42:6**

Comfort ye, comfort ye my people, saith your God. Speak ye comfortably to Jerusalem, and cry unto her, that her warfare is accomplished, that her iniquity is pardoned: for she hath received of the LORD's hand double for all her sins. **Isa 40:1-2**

Remember ye not the former things, neither consider the things of old. Behold, I will do a new thing; now it shall spring forth; shall ye not know it? I will even make a way in the wilderness, and rivers in the desert. **Isa. 43:18-19**

Remember these, O Jacob and Israel; for thou art my servant: I have formed thee; thou art my servant: O Israel, thou shalt not be forgotten of me; I have blotted out, as a thick cloud, thy transgressions, and, as a cloud, thy sins: return unto me; for I have redeemed thee. **Isa. 44:21-22**

I will go before thee, and make the crooked places straight: I will break in pieces the gates of brass, and cut in sunder the bars of iron: And I will give thee the treasures of darkness, and hidden riches of secret places, that thou mayest know that I, the LORD, which call thee by thy name, am the God of Israel. **Isa. 45:2-3**

Thus saith the LORD, In an acceptable time have I heard thee, and in a day of salvation have I helped thee: and I will preserve thee, and give thee for a covenant of the people, to establish the earth, to cause to inherit the desolate heritages; That thou mayest say to the prisoners, Go forth; to them that are in darkness, Shew yourselves. They shall feed in the ways, and their pastures shall be in all high places. They shall not hunger not thirst; neither shall the heat nor sun smite them: for he that hath mercy on them shall lead them, even by the springs of water shall he guide them. Isa. 49:8-10

Can a woman forget her sucking child, that she should not have compassion on the son of her womb? yea, they may forget, yet will I not forget thee. Behold, I have graven thee upon the palms of my hands; thy walls are continually before me. Thy Children shall make haste; thy destroyers and they that made thee waste shall go forth of thee. **Isa. 49:15-17**

Behold, the Lord GOD will help me; who is he that shall condemn me? lo, they all shall wax old as a garment; the moth shall eat them up. **Isaiah 50:9**

No weapon that is formed against thee shall prosper; and every tongue that shall rise against thee in judgment thou shalt condemn. This is the heritage of the servants of the LORD, and their righteousncss is of me, saith the LORD. **Isaiah 54:17**

Arise, shine; for thy light is come, and the glory of the LORD is risen upon thee. For, behold, the darkness shall cover the earth, and gross darkness the people: but the LORD shall arise upon thee, and his glory shall be seen upon thee.

And the Gentiles shall come to thy light, and kings to the brightness of thy rising. Lift up thine eyes round about, and see: all they gather themselves together, they come to thee: thy sons shall come from far, and thy daughters shall be nursed at thy side. Then thou shalt see, and flow together, and thine heart shall fear, and be enlarged; because the abundance of the sea shall be converted unto thee, the forces of the Gentiles shall come unto thee. The multitude of camels shall cover thee, the dromedaries of Midian and Ephah; all they from Sheba shall come: they shall bring gold and incense; and they shall shew forth the praises of the LORD. All the flocks of Kedar shall he gathered together unto thee, the rams of Nebaioth shall minister unto thee: they shall come up with acceptance on mine altar, and I will glorify the house of my glory Isa. 60:1-7

And strangers shall stand and feed your flocks, and the sons of the alien shall be your plowmen and your vinedressers. But ye shall be named the Priests of the LORD: men shall call you the Ministers of our God: ye shall eat the riches of the Gentiles, and in their glory shall ye boast yourselves. For your shame ye shall have double; and for confusion they shall rejoice in their portion: therefore in their land they shall possess the double: everlasting joy shall be unto them.
Isa. 61:5-7

Meditate on these scriptures and assurance will flood your heart. One thing we need to know is that; God says what He means and He means what He says. When you meditate upon His word, your faith will be built up. You will be encouraged and God will give you fresh assurances. Your life will echo the words of a songwriter.

Great is Thy faithfulness. O God my Father;
There is no shadow of turning with Thee;
Thou changest not, Thy compassions, they fail not;
As thou hast been, Thou forever will be.

Great is Thy faithfulness!
Great is Thy faithfulness!
Morning by morning new mercies I see.
All I have needed Thy hand hath provided;
Great is Thy faithfulness, Lord, unto me!

Summer and winter and springtime and harvest,
Sun, moon and stars in their courses above
Join with all nature in manifold witness
To Thy great faithfulness, mercy and love.

Pardon for sin and a peace that endureth
Thine own dear presence to cheer and to guide;
Strength for today and bright hope for tomorrow
Blessings all mine, with ten thousand beside!

FRESH ASSURANCE

May God give you fresh assurances today. May His truth be your shield and buckler. May His word inspire confidence in you. May His gentle voice drown every form of discouragement disturbing your inner mind. May His words motivate you, His thoughts transform you and His promises renew your strength.

Beloved, it is well with your soul. Your story shall change, your Goliath shall be disgraced, your Red

Sea shall dry up. Your stubborn pursuers shall die by fire. God will prove Himself in your life. He will defend His interest in you. He will prove to the whole world that He is the God who answereth by fire. God shall visit you and He shall make everything beautiful in His time.

NOTES:

_____

_____

_____

_____

_____

_____

_____

_____

_____

_____

_____

_____

_____

_____

_____

_____

_____

_____

_____

_____

_____

_____

_____

Chapter 12

THE
RESTORING
VOICE

The voice of God is the voice of confidence. Confidence is akin to assurance but differs in one way or the other. The root of the word confidence is trust or believing in someone's ability. You need the voice of confidence for two purposes. You need it to have confidence in your own God-given ability. The need for self esteem is important today. Rather than manifest self esteem, people go about with an abysmal poor opinion concerning themselves. Some people lack confidence in themselves to the extent that they are scared in attempting any new venture. Even when they are doing what is right, they refrain from going further because they are scared that people may cast on them a vote of no confidence. Others are not moving forward at all because of lack of confidence in God.

The greatest damage you can do against yourself is to allow your confidence in God to be eroded. Why must we lack confidence in the Almighty? Why should we allow the circumstances of life to puncture your confidence in God?

> *Cast not away therefore your confidence, which hath great recompence of reward. For ye have need of patience, that, after ye have done the will of God, ye*

*might receive the promise. For yet
a little while, and he that shall
come will come, and will not tarry.
Now the just shall live by faith: but
if any men draw back, my soul
shall have no pleasure in him. But
we are not of them who drawback
unto perdition; but of them that
believe to the saving of the soul.*
Heb. 10:35-39

Why don't you manifest unwavering faith in God?
God wants to build up your confidence so that you
can dare circumstances and situations knowing that
greater is he who lives in you than he who lives in the
world.

Ye are of God, little children, and have overcome
them: because greater is he that is in you, than he that
is in the world. 1 John 4:4

THE VOICE OF RESTORATION

The voice of God is the voice of restoration. Our
experience in the deliverance ministry shows that the
devil is a thief who specialises in stealing every good
thing in the life of people. Hence, many people have
experienced colossal losses in several departments of

their lives. This loss has made people to live empty lives. The substance is gone. All they have is the carcass. The only word that can describe the situation of men and women today is the word Ichcahod.

> *And she named the child*
> *Ichabod, saying, The glory is*
> *departed from Israel: because*
> *the ark of God was taken, and*
> *because of her father in law and*
> *her husband. 1 Sam. 4:21*

When the glory departs, every other attempt made to achieve anything will end in futility. Lives will be shallow destinies will be emptied and glories will be turned to shame. What we need today is the voice of restoration.

AREAS OF RESTORATION

The Bible has outlined the following areas of restoration.

1. Restoration of destiny
2. Restoration of lost glory
3. Restoration of power
4. Ministerial restoration
5. Marriage restoration
6. Career restoration

7. Restoration of backsliders
8. Total restoration
9. Restoration of what your ancestors lost
10. Restoration of dignity
11. Restoration of anointing
12. Restoration of blessings
13. Restoration of divine positions
14. Restoration of divine presence
15. Restoration of the divine programme for your life.
16. Restoration of divine benefits
17. Restoration of lost divine connections.
18. Restoration of lost opportunities.
19. Restoration of wealth.
20. Restoration of health
21. Restoration of promotion
22. Restoration of spiritual gifts
23. Restoration of divine confidence and assurance
24. Restoration of healing
25. Restoration of talents and divine skills
26. Restoration of joy
27. Restoration of peace
28. Restoration of open doors

DISCOVER TO RECOVER

You need the voice of restoration to experience total revival, rejuvenation and resurrection in the above listed areas. This is the season of restoration. This is the hour of renewal. This is the moment of taking back what the enemy has stolen. Now is the time to discover to recover and possess your possessions in Christ. God's promises are sure.

> *And I will restore to you the years that the locust hath eaten, the cankerworm, and the caterpiller, and the palmerworm, my great army which I sent among you.*
> *Joel 2:25*

> *For I will restore health unto thee, and I will heal thee of thy wounds, saith the LORD; because they called thee an Outcast, saying, This is Zion, whom no man seeketh after Jer. 30:17*

> *And I will restore thy judges as at the first, and thy counsellors as at the beginning: afterward thou shalt be called, The city of righteousness, the faithful city Isa. 1:26*

What we need today is the voice of complete restoration which will fully restore the totality of our lives and destiny and make our lives glorify His name and honour His majesty.

VOICE OF PROMOTION

The voice of God is the voice of promotion. Life is not static. We need to make progress in order to find fulfilment in God. If what you were some years ago is what you are at the moment, it leaves much to be desired. If you have been standing still for several years without any appreciable promotion or movement from one level to another, it shows that you are yet lo hear the voice of promotion.

The voice of promotion comes from God, when He asks you to move from one level to another level, when you can see a remarkable difference from what you used to be and to what you have become.

AREAS OF PROMOTION

Promotion can be experienced in many areas of life. This includes.

1. Academic promotion
2. Career promotion.
3. Official promotion.
4. Ministerial promotion
5. Promotion in the area of your status.
6. Promotion occurs when a bachelor or a spinster gets married.
7. When couples become parents.

8. When employees become employers.
9. When debtors become creditors.
10. When tenants become home owners.
11. When jobless graduates become gainfully employed.
12. When servants become masters.
13. When youths become leaders.

THE SOURCE OF PROMOTION

There are other areas where we can witness remarkable promotion and people will begin to give glory to God. The voice of promotion can only sound from the throne of God. Unless God promotes you nobody can promote you. When you seek promotion from man, you may end up being promoted out of relevance. But God's promotion will surely make you to become the type of person God wants you to be.

The Bible says;

> For promotion cometh neither from the east, nor from the west, nor from the south. But God is the judge: he putteth down one, and setteth up another. **Ps. 75:6-7**

THE HOLY PROMOTER

God is a God of promotion. He can promote you by taking you out of the prison to the palace after the order of Joseph. He can move you from the status of a slave and make you a vice-president after the order of Daniel. He can move you from an ordinary person to the status of a queen after the order of Esther. There is nothing God cannot do. He can make a servant to ride upon horses. He can pick you from the gutter and position you in a palace. God is the one who promotes.

It is my prayer that God will promote you by fire and settle you in your high places.

You need the voice of promotion to experience a shift that is so significant that people will begin to wonder. When God promotes you, people will stare at you in wonder when they consider how you have made a sudden jump from the lowest wrung to the highest wrung of the ladder.

NOTES:

_____

_____

_____

_____

_____

_____

_____

_____

_____

_____

_____

_____

_____

_____

_____

_____

_____

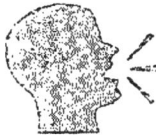

Chapter 13
THE VOICE
OF
DELIVERANCE

God's voice is the voice of deliverance. The world in which we live is a battle ground. A lot of people have received arrows of bondage. Many have been battered as a result of attacks from the kingdom of darkness. A lot of people are victims of lost glory stolen virtues and exchanged virtues. Many people have suffered terrible pain and agony due to satanic bondage, jinxes, arrows of darkness, curses, unbroken covenants and attacks from household witchcraft and the powers of the emptiers. Hence, a lot of people are victims of satanic bondage.

The voice of deliverance is one voice we need desperately today.

WHEN YOU NEED THE VOICE OF DELIVERANCE

The following cases need the voice of deliverance.

1. Arrows of bondage
2. Attacks from witchcraft
3. Stolen virtues
4. Ancestral bondage
5. Failure at the edge of miracles
6. Attacks from the powers of the emptiers
7. Arrows of limitations
8. Victims of "You Shall Not Get There" curses

9. Arrows of falling from great heights
10. Arrows of moving about in circles
11. Arrows of miscarriage
12. Arrows of insanity
13. Arrows of mistakes
14. Arrows of foolishness
15. Arrows of fatal accidents
16. Victims basking in yesterdays glory
17. Victims of marital failure
18. Arrows of inability to get married at all
19. Arrows of childlessness
20. The poison of backwardness
21. The jinx of abandoned projects
22. The syndrome of come back next time
23. The problem of demonic manipulation
24. The problem of repeated failure
25. The arrow of constant tragedies
26. The arrow of cyclical misfortune
27. Attacks from the womb
28. Curse of failure
29. Victims of destiny amputators
30. The arrow of moving to dry places
31. The arrow of rejection and hatred
32. Arrow of remaining at the tail region
33. Arrow of disgrace
34. Arrow of wickedness
35. Arrow of powerlessness

36. Arrow of nakedness
37. Arrow of insanity
38. Arrow of stagnation
39. Arrow of poverty
40. The victim syndrome
41. Arrow of walking into danger
42. Arrow of constant bad luck
43. Arrow of being the scapegoat
44. Family failure
45. Career failure
46. Arrow of procrastination of good things.
47. Arrow of nightmares
48. Arrow of terrible dream attacks
49. Arrow of incurable diseases
50. Arrow of bedwetting
51. Arrows of being the laughing stock
52. Arrows of working like an elephant but eating like an ant
53. Arrows of lateness in getting to a place of blessings
54. Arrows of being absent when angels of blessings arrive
55. Arrows of idolatry
56. Arrows of household wickedness
57. Arrows of unfriendly friend
58. Arrows of evil broadcasts
59. Arrows of attacks coming from fake prophets
60. Arrows of impossibilities

THE VOICE OF POWER

These and other problems need a great voice from heaven and the only voice that can put a stop to these nagging problems is the voice of deliverance. The voice of deliverance is the voice of power. It is the voice that cannot be resisted. It is the voice that sounds like thunder and lightening. When the voice of deliverance sounds, evil spirits will summersault and "die". Satanic agents will be disgraced and emissaries of darkness will take a flight. When demonic powers attack you one way the voice of deliverance will make them to flee in seven ways.

The voice of deliverance is the voice of the God who answers by fire. A lot of people whose destinies have been rubbished have lived glorious lives. After deliverance comes fulfilment. After deliverance comes rest. After deliverance comes the emergence of your glory: Deliverance will make you to shine like a star. Deliverance will enable you to possess your possessions.

> *But upon mount Zion shall be deliverance, and there shall be holiness; and the house off Jacob shall possess their possessions.*
> **Obadiah 1:17**

We need the voice of deliverance today

The Spirit of the Lord is upon me, because he hath anointed me to preach the gospel to the poor; he hath sent me to heal the brokenhearted, to preach deliverance to the captives, and recovering of sight to the blind, to set at liberty them that are bruised, *Luke 4:18*

NOTES:

Chapter 14

THE VOICE
OF
FRUITFULNESS

T he voice of God is the voice of fruitfulness. The problem of fruitless hard work is a prevalent problem in our society. Fruitlessness is not of God. At the beginning of creation, God issued a command.

> *And God blessed them, saying, Be fruitful, and multiply; and fill the waters in the seas, and let fowl multiply in the earth.* **Gen. 1:22**

That voice of fruitfulness that sounded at the beginning of creation will sound upon your life and your destiny and you shall be fruitful in the name of Jesus.

IMPORTANT AREAS

You need fruitfulness in the following areas.

1. Fruitfulness in business.
2. The fruit of the womb
3. Fruitfulness in ministry
4. Fruitfulness in your spiritual life
5. Fruitfulness in life's endeavour
6. Fruitfulness in your academic work
7. Fruitfulness among your colleagues
8. Fruitfulness in your work place
9. Fruitfulness in your prayer ministry
10. Fruitfulness in the area of evangelism

11.   Fruitfulness in church planting and growth
12.   Fruitfulness in the area of prosperity
13.   Fruitfulness at home
14.   Fruitfulness at work
15.   Fruitfulness in the farm

God's promise of fruitfulness rings out powerfully in the passage below

> *And all these blessings shall come on, thee, and overtake thee, if thou shalt hearken unto the voice of the LORD thy God. Blessed shalt thou be in the city and blessed shalt thou be in the field. Blessed shall be the fruit of thy body and the fruit of thy ground, and the fruit of thy cattle, the increase of thy kine, and the flocks of thy sheep. Blessed shall be thy basket and thy store. Blessed shalt thou be when thou comest in, and blessed shalt thou be when thou goest out.*
> ***Deut 28:2-6***

IMPORTANT STEPS

However, there is a part you need to play if you want to be fruitful. You must take the following steps.

1. Obey the word of God.
2. Repent of every form of disobedience
3. Obey God's word on giving and tithing. If you want God to speak the voice of fruitfulness you need to be a tither. When you support God's cause on earth, He will support your cause. Someone has humorously said it this way; "If you shovel up to God, He will shovel back to you". When you give to God, you will end up supporting the work of the ministry

As the emphasis of the Church is on missions at the moment, we need a lot of money to send missionaries to various countries of the world. Churches will be planted, converts will be discipled, workers will be trained, villages will be reached, and urban centres will witness the saving power of the Lord Jesus Christ. The church will spend quite a lot of money on these glorious projects. Since evangelism is the heartbeat of the Almighty and missions is the pulse of the heart of God, God is going to bless covenant givers who will surrender themselves

PROSPERITY SECRETS

When you give, God will give back to you

> *Give, and it shall be given unto you; good measure, pressed down, and shaken together, and running over, shall men give into your bosom. For with the same measure that ye mete withal it shall, be measured to you again.*
> ***Luke 6:38***

He will not only give you the measure you gave to him, He will give you more, press down, shaken together and running over. God will always exceed whatever you give Him.

WHAT YOU CAN DO

Practically speaking, your giving will do the following things in the church.

1.   There will be meat in God's house
2.   The Gospel of the kingdom shall be preached
3.   Ministers shall be taken care of
4.   Projects shall be financed (e.g. the Deliverance Stadium and giving the International Headquarters a befitting status).

5. Fund for missions
6. Support for ministerial schools
7. Funds for hosting training programmes and international conferences.
8. The General Overseer's welfare

9. Payment of the rent for the church premises and the rates and levies as demanded by the locality
10. Purchasing and maintaining a pool of cars and vehicles for the church
11. Purchasing vehicles for branches, church staffs and ministers
12. Payment of the electricity bills and the purchase of diesel for generator during church services
13. Cost of travel for programmes, crusades, deliverance programmes, anointing services and training programmes in MFM branches at home and abroad.
14. Financing the repair and maintenance of new and existing church branches and their structures

The list is almost inexhaustible. Therefore, when you give you gladden the heart of God. When you support his cause on earth, He blesses you. According to our ancient Fathers money is the wheel of the gospel. This claim is supported by the scriptures.

The God's prosperity plan for this end time is to make His children rich. This can only happen when you are an incurable giver and you support the work; of the gospel.

YOU CAN MAKE A DIFFERENCE

Do you know that your giving can make a difference? Do you know that you can inspire the voice of fruitfulness when you give in such a manner as to make God happy? Remember, the commandments and promises of God;

> *Give, and it shall be given unto you; good measure, pressed down, and shaken together, and running over, shall men give into your bosom. For with the same measure that ye mete withal it shall be measured to you again.* **Luke 6:38**

> *Bring ye all the tithes into the storehouse, that there may be meat in mine house, and prove me now herewith, saith the LORD of hosts, if I will not open you the windows of heaven, and pour you*

*out a blessing, that there shall not
be room enough to receive it.*
Malachi 3:10

I give glory to God for men and women who have discovered the power of fruitfulness. By giving, they have provoked God to utter the voice of fruitfulness.

The moment this voice sounds in your life, people will begin to wonder what exactly is the source of your prosperity and blessing. Be a giver today and God will surprise you.

NOTES:

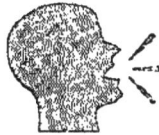

Chapter 15

THE VOICE
OF
GLORY

The voice of God is the voice of favour. There is nothing as good as being favoured by the Almighty. When you are favoured, God will make you a recipient of His blessings. He will single you out for uncommon blessings. Favour will envelope you with the flavour of glory. You will be uniquely blessed, as the voice of the Almighty will locate you within the crowd and the ornament of favour will distinguish you as someone who has been divinely chosen by God. When you attempt any venture, favour will make you to succeed. Favour will transform your life. You need the voice of favour today.

THE VOICE OF HONOUR

The voice of God is the voice of honour and glory. Honour comes from God, Glory cannot be bought with money but when God speaks honour and glory into your life, your life will become glorious.

God can pick up a nonentity and speak the word of honour and glory into his life

> *For the LORD God is a sun and shield: the LORD will give grace and glory: no good thing will he withhold from them that walk uprightly.* **Psalm 84:11**

The voice of God is the voice of honour. When He speaks to you no one can dishonour you. When He speaks, no power can rubbish your glory His glory will overshadow you and His voice will lavish divine glory upon your life and destiny Let God speak into your life with the voice of honour today and you will never remain the same.

THE VOICE OF DIVINE REST

The voice of God is the voice of divine rest. We all stand in need of peace in a world ravaged by trouble. All over the world people are suffering from chaos, arguments, frequent squabbles, riots, family feuds and communal clashes. Restfulness is the greatest need of our present generation. Incidentally the more people search for peace or rest the more it eludes them.

> *They have healed also the hurt of the daughter of my people slightly, saying, Peace, peace; when there is no peace.* **Jeremiah 6:14**

A lot of peace treaties have been signed, many communiques have been issued, yet, the world is yet to witness true peace. Jesus is the prince of peace. There can be no peace in the world until He commences His eternal reign. However, when you begin to allow him reign in your life a regime of peace has started within you.

Jesus came to the world to usher in an era of peace

> *For unto us a child is born, unto us a son is given: and the government shall be upon his shoulder: and his name shall be called Wonderful, Counsellor, The mighty God, The everlasting Father, The Prince of Peace. Isaiah 9:6*

GREAT PEACE!

The Prince of Peace will speak with the voice of peace and you shall experience peace in the following areas

1. Peace in your soul
2. Peace when you go to Calvary with the guilt of your sins
3. Peace in your work place
4. Peace in the family
5. Peace in the Church
6. Peace when you are bombarded by trouble from every angle
7. Peace when creditors bombard you reminding of unpaid debts

8. Peace when there are wars within and without
9. Peace when trouble brews within the family
10. Peace when the enemy threatens you

These and other situations will make the God of peace arise and bruise Satan under your feet.

> *And the God of peace shall bruise Satan under your feet shortly. The grace of our Lord Jesus Christ be with you, Amen.* **Romans 16:20**

God will speak the word of peace into your life. God will bombard you with peace like a river.

> *For thus saith the LORD, Behold, I will extend peace to her like a river, and the glory of the Gentiles like a flowing stream: then shall ye suck, ye shall be borne upon her sides, and be dandled upon her knees.* **Isaiah 66:12**

What we are looking into in this area; concerns how God responds, when we depend upon His promise. God is our creator. We depend on him for provision, sustenance, help, grace and stability. We go through a lot in this world that none of us can-survive. God knows the length and breadth as will as the beginning and the end. He knows what we will go through regardless of where we find ourselves. Hence, He has given us thousands of promise.

> *Whereby are given unto us exceeding great and precious promises: that by these ye might be partakers of the divine nature, having escaped the corruption that is in the world through lust.* **2 Peter 1:4**

GREAT PROMISES

The subject of promises needs to be addressed here. There are over seven thousand promises in the word of God. It is also interesting to note that, there are three hundred and sixty six fear-not in the Bible. This shows that there is a fear-not for each day; either it is a leap year or a normal year. There is no dening the fact that God has given us great and precious promises.

These promises are real. The beauty of the promises of God is that, each time we take them to God in prayer, God has only one response, he simply says

*For all the promises of God in him
are yea, and in him Amen, unto
the glory of God by us.* **2
Corinthians 1:20**

GOD SAYS YES

Hence, the voice of God is the voice of yea and
Amen. In other words when you remind God of what
He has promised you, He simply says yes and so let it
be. God does not say no to His promises. He does
not renege on His word.

*If we believe not, yet he abideth
faithful: he cannot deny himself.* **2
Timothy 2:13**

There are lots of things to explore as far as the voice of
God is concerned. When you immerse your self in
the river of the voice of God, other negative voices
will fade into insignificance. Plunge yourself into the
divine voice today and negative voices will find no
place in your life.

Chapter 16

THE TRAGEDY
OF
NEGATIVE
VOICES

There are many types of voices in the world. Some are positive and others are negative. There are voices that can add positive values to your life while some voices can bring problems and sorrow into your life. When some voices come into your life, there will be order, peace and stability. When other voices come into your life, they bring chaos, sorrow and calamity.

NEGATIVE PATTERNS

It is your duty therefore, to watch the type of voice you allow to penetrate into your life and destiny. When we talk of negative voices, they are characterized by the following.

1. Confusing voices
2. Conflicting voices
3. Voices that derail
4. Voices that make you doubt God's word
5. Voices that drag into worldliness and sin
6. Voices that make people to go into unhealthy comparison
7. Voices that program negative thoughts into people's lives
8. Voices that make you contemplate suicide
9. Voices that negatively inspire people to forsake the way of the Lord by joining the band wagon

10. Voices that lead into insanity
11. Voices that lead to backsliding
12. Voices that make believers put one leg in the Church and another in the world
13. Voices that tell people that holiness is impossible
14. Voices that lead to compromise
15. Voices that compel people to go into compulsive negative attitudes
16. Voices that compel people to take dangerous actions
17. Voices that trigger mental imbalance
18. Voices that compel people to gang up against their leaders in the church
19. Voices that inspire people to join the wrong majority
20. Voices that compel youths to copy the latest worldly trends and fashions
21. Voices that compel people to follow the example of Judas
22. Voices that compel people to follow the example of Eve
23. Voices that tell people to follow the example of Gehazi
24. Voices that inspire people to follow the pattern of Cain
25. Voice that call on people to follow the greed of Balaam

26. Voices that inspire people to follow the pattern of Judas who betrayed his Lord
27. Voices that lure people to follow the example of Demas who loved the world and turned away from following the Lord
28. Voices that tell people to follow the example of king Saul. Who disobeyed the voice of the Lord and chose the path of disobedience which can be likened to witchcraft
29. Voices that tell ladies to copy the character of Jezebel
30. Voices that lure men and women into idol worship, in the name of preserving the culture of their ancestors
31. Voices that tell people that nothing is wrong with a little compromise
32. Voices that tell people to adopt a hypocritical lifestyle that will make them smart.

The list of negative voices is endless. One thing is clear; negative voices inspire negative actions and lead to negative results. You cannot close your eyes as if there are no negative voices. Unfortunately; negative voices are louder than positive ones.

Voices from the camp of the enemy come from every angle, at home, in the office, in the church and in schools. Negative voices are sounding every moment. If God can open your eyes to the damaging effects of negative voices, you will decide to shut your ears lest your destiny is affected by voices from the kingdom of darkness.

NEGATIVE VOICES

> *There are lots of negative voices that mislead people. We must shun these voices. Remember; there are, it may be, so many kinds of voices in the world, and none of them is without signification.* **1 Cor. 14:10,**

This verse establishes the fact that, whether we like it or not there are many types of voices. Some voices are sent to do good while others are sent to perpetuate evil. Each voice has a mission. Each voice has an agenda. It takes a discerning mind to identify and distinguish between good and bad voices.

> *And when he putteth forth his own sheep, he goeth before them, and the sheep follow him: for they know his voice, and a stranger will they not follow; but will flee from him: for they know not the voice of strangers.* **John 10:4-5**

TWO VOICES

Again, we are told that there are two types of voices; The voice of the shepherd and that of the stranger. Those who follow the shepherd will listen to His voice. However, those who are not part of the sheep will follow the voice of the stranger. The one whom you follow will reveal whether you are a sheep or a goat. Sheep follow the shepherd, goats follow strangers.

There are many voices in the world. People are known by their voices. Voices can be likened to means of identification of the kind of person you are. There are characteristics of voices to consider, we shall examine them in this chapter. People can be recognised by their voices though, some people often try to disguise.

Voices carry messages. Voices can be imitated. There is a story in the Old Testament that shows that people often tend to change their voices to conceal their identity. I want you to read the story.

> *At that time Ahijah the son of Jeroboam fell sick. And Jeroboam said to his wife, Arise, I pray thee, and disguise thyself,*

that thou be not known to be the wife of Jeroboam; and get thee to Shiloh: behold, there is Ahijah the prophet, which told me that I should be king over this people. And take with thee ten loaves, and cracknels, and a cruse of honey and go to him: he shall tell thee what shall become of the child. And Jeroboam's wife did so, and arose, and went to Shiloh, and came to the house of Ahijah. But Ahijah could not see; for his eyes were set by reason of his age. And the LORD said unto Ahijah, Behold, the wife of Jeroboam cometh to ask a thing of thee for her son; for he is sick: thus and thus shalt thou say unto her: for it shall be, when she cometh in, that she shall feign herself to be another woman. And it was so, when Ahijah heard the sound of her feet as she came in at the door that he said, Come in, thou wife of Jeroboam; why feignest thou thyself to be another? For I am sent to thee with heavy tidings. **1 Kings 14:1-6**

DECEPTION GALORE

The prophet of God Ahijah had become blind due to old age. Though his physical eyes had become blind, his spiritual eyes were extremely sharp. The wife acted the script perfectly. But unknown to her, God had told the prophet that she would come in and try to change her voice to appear as someone else. Although the woman changed her voice but the voice with which God created her remained with her.

What we can learn here is that your voice is your real identity even if you try to imitate someone else's voice. The woman tried to put up a voice to deceive the prophet but the Spirit of God revealed her true voice.

Voices reveal certain information. Voices portray people's true identity. Voices give out the kind of person you are. Apart from your own individual voice, you hear voices all the time in the following situations.

1. When neighbours and friends speak to you
2. When you listen to strangers and casual acquaintances

3. When you listen to the voice of your co-workers and neighbours
4. When you listen to the voices of your enemies
5. When you listen to voices through the media (Newspapers, radio, TV.)

NOTES:

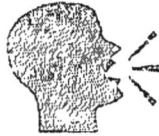

Chapter 17

DOMINION OVER NEGATIVE VOICES

The voice of the LORD breaketh the cedars; yea, the LORD breaketh the cedars of Lebanon.
Psalm 29:5

We hear voices all the time. However, hearing is one thing, listening and accepting what is heard is another thing. When people talk, you hear because it is virtually impossible to block your ears. But one power which you have is the power to sift and choose what you want to accept in spite of the numerous things which has found its way into your life through your ear drums.

We must sort out voices, identify the strange ones and overpower them. For the purpose of clarity we need to identify the fact that there are both internal and external voices. However, the voice that affects mankind most is the inner voice. The inner voice may not be loud; but it is loaded with power because it comes from within.

The spirit of man is the candle of the LORD, searching all the inward parts of the belly **Prov. 20:27**

THE INNER VOICE

We need to pay attention to the power of the inner voice. This is because internal negative voices have turned many lives upside down. The power of the inner voice was brought to the fore during Paul's journey as recorded below

> *And when it was determined that we should sail into Italy; they delivered Paul and certain other prisoners unto one named Julius, a centurion of Augustus' band. And entering into a ship of Adramyttium, we launched, meaning to sail by the coasts of Asia; one Aristarchus, a Macedonian of Thessalonica, being with us. And the next day we touched at Sidon. And Julius courteously entreated Paul, and gave him liberty to go unto his friends to refresh himself. And when we had launched from thence, we sailed under Cyprus, because the winds were contrary. And when we had sailed over the sea of Cilicia and Pamphylia, we came to Myra, a city of Lycia. And there the centurion*

found a ship of Alexandria sailing into Italy; and he put us therein. And when we had sailed slowly many days, and scarce were come over against Cnidus, the wind not suffering us, we sailed under Crete, over against Salmone; And, hardly passing it, came unto a place which is called The fair havens; nigh whereunto was the city of`Lasea. Now when much time was spent, and when sailng was now dangerous, because the fast was now already past, Paul admonished them, And said unto them, Sirs, I perceive that this voyage will be with hurt and much damage, not only of the lading and ship, but also of our lives. Nevertheless the centurion believed the master and the owner of the ship, more than those things which were spoken by Paul. Acts 27:1-11,

And when neither sun nor stars in many days appeared, and no small tempest lay on us, all hope that we should be saved was then taken away. But after long abstinence Paul stood forth in the midst of them, and said, Sirs, ye should have hearkened unto me, and not have loosed from Crete, and to have gained this harm and loss. And now I exhort you to be of good cheer: for there shall be no loss of any man's life among you, but of the ship. For there stood by me this night the angel of God, whose I am, and whom I serve, Saying, Fear not, Paul; thou must be brought before Caesar: and, lo, God hath given thee all them that sail with thee. Wherefore, sirs, be of good cheer: for I believe God, that it shall be even as it was told me. Howbeit we must be cast upon a certain island. But when the fourteenth night was come, as we were driven up and down in Adria, about midnight the shipmen deemed that they drew near to some country; And *sounded, and found it twenty fathoms: and when they had gone a little further; they sounded again, and found it fifteen fathoms. Then fearing lest we should have fallen upon rocks, they cast four anchors out of the stern, and wished for the day. And as the shipmen were about to flee out of the ship, when they had let down the boat into the sea, under colour as though they would have cast anchors out of the foreship, Paul said to the centurion and to the soldiers, Except these abide in the ship, ye cannot be saved. Then the soldiers cut off the ropes of the boat, and let her fall off. And while the day was coming on, Paul besought them all to take meat, saying, This day is the fourteenth day that ye have tarried and continued fasting, having taken nothing. Wherefore I pray you to take some meat: for this is for your health: for there shall not an hair fall from the head of any of you. And when he had thus spoken, he took bread, and gave thanks to God in presence of them all: and when he had broken it, he began to eat. Then were they all of good cheer and they also took some meat. And we were in all in the ship two hundred threescore and sixteen souls. And when they had eaten enough, they lightened the ship, and Cast out the wheat into the sea. And when it was day, they knew not the land: but they discovered a certain creek with a shore, in to the which they were minded, if it were possible, to thrust in the ship. And when they had taken up the anchors, they committed themselves unto the sea, and loosed the rudder bands, and hoised up the mainsail to the wind, and made toward shore. And falling into a place where two seas met, they ran the ship aground; and the forepart stuck fast, and remained unmovable, but the hinder part was broken with the violence of the waves. And the soldiers' counsel was to kill the prisoners, lest any of them should swim out, and escape. But the centurion, willing to save Paul, kept them from their purpose; and commanded that they which could swim should cast themselves first into the sea, and get to land: And the rest, some on boards, and some on broken pieces of the ship. And so it came to pass, that they escaped all safe to land.* **Acts 27:20-44**

TWO MAJOR CHARACTERS

The above story presents two major characters. Here we have two major voices. The voice of man and voice of God. Julius represents the voice of man while Paul represents the voice of God. Paul the Apostle perceived that there would be danger during the journey but the centurion believed the master and owner of the ship more than the words of Paul.

In every situation in which we are faced with two choices, we either believe the voice of man or believe the voice of God. At the end of the day the voice of God prevailed over the voice of man.

> And said unto them, Sirs, I perceive that this voyage will be with hurt and much damage, not only of the lading and ship, but also of our lives. Nevertheless the centurion believed the master and the owner of the ship, more than those things which were spoken by Paul. **Acts 27:10-11**

> But after long abstinence Paul stood forth in the midst of them, and said, Sirs, ye should have hearkened unto me, and not have loosed from Crete, and to have gained this harm and loss. **Acts 27:21**

Although, Paul alerted his fellow travellers but they decided to listen to another voice. However, they learnt their lessons. Just as Paul told them that there shall be no loss of any man's life, no life was lost.

> And now I exhort you to be of good cheer: for there shall be no loss of any man's life among you, but of the ship. **Acts 27:22**

*And the rest, some on boards, and
some on broken pieces of the ship.
And so it came to pass, that they
escaped all safe to land.* **Acts 27:44**

Here, we discover one important fact. What we hear
does not really matter. It is what we accept that
matters. As long as we remain alive, we shall always
be faced with two choices, either to embrace the
voice of God or accept the voice of man.

No man can please God on the basis of natural
observation; neither can we walk with God on the
basis of common sense. The word of man will lead
you astray. The words of God will direct you to the
right path. Human opinion will fail but God's word
will prevail.

NOTES:

Chapter 18

THE COMPELLING NEGATIVE VOICES

I t is unfortunate, however, that people now believe the media than what God says. Here is a great truth to consider. Not everything within a man is in total support or in agreement with either God or Satan. However, the moment you are able to discern correctly you will be able to manage every voice trying to gain entry into your life.

The truth is that the battle with voices takes place within. It is not really an external battle. The moment you conquer the internal battle, external battles become a walk over. If you loose the inner battle, you will surely loose the external battle.

The tragedy of the modern day generation is that, people are no longer ready. listen to "Thus saith the Lord". People would rather listen to what can be proved scientifically and what is in line with human reckoning. Let me make this clear to you. Many people are grappling with problems and tragedies today simply because they paid attention to dark words.

COMMON VOICES

These are the common voices that influence us.

1. The voice of God,
2. The voice of the devil

3. Parent's voices
4. Children voices
5. Peer's voices
6. Gossip's voices
7. Voices of those sent on satanic assignment
8. Lying voices
9. Hypocritical voices
10. Voices of false prophets'
11. Voices of agents of darkness
12. Voices of unfriendly friends
13. Voices of those who distort the truth
14. Voices of those who fabricate lies
15. Voices of those who try to provoke you
16. Voices of workers of iniquity
17. Voices of evil counsellors
18. Voices of those who claim to know everything because of age and experience
19. Voices of forgers of lies and physicians of no value.

AUDIBLE VOICES

Besides these voices, some people hear audible demonic voices. The voices tell them to harm themselves, destroy things or go into highly demonic acts. There are voices that human beings can hardly recognise but these voices speak powerfully. Some voices are so subtle that we can easily ignore them but the words they speak can become very destructive. Your best friend can speak innocently and lead you astray

Again, the mirror may appear insignificant, but it speaks powerfully when you take a look at the mirror you often lower your guards since you are simply admiring yourself. The mirror will not only give you a picture of yourself, it will come up with a voice, some mild suggestions.

THE POWER OF THE MIRROR

The mirror may tell you; why don't you compete with your neighbour who has a set of dazzling white teeth? Why don't you go to a special beauty parlour where you can white wash your teeth and look flashy again?" Again, the mirror may tell you; "Look at your hairstyle; it is out of tune with latest trend? Why don't you acquire the latest weave-on and style your hair the way people in the world do?"

The mirror may also tell you, just take a look at your complexion, it has become so dull; you have completely lost your shine. Buy an expensive cream and tone up a little. You can go for a whitening using expensive bleaching chemicals. The mirror will also tell you to conform your shape and style with what is in vogue." It will then make a subtle suggestion saying that you should make yourself attractive a little. By the time you are through with listening to the voice of the mirror, you will begin to embrace worldliness gradually.

A POWERFUL VOICE

The voice of the mirror is a voice that is as close to you as your skin. It is there with you in your house, even when you shut your doors against your neighbours and friends, your mirror voice will penetrate into your ears. You will find yourself listening to the voice of your mirror.

Your mirror has a voice, it speaks. It instructs. It is unfortunate that the mirror is not a servant. It is a very wicked master. Though, may show you your true picture, it would tell you that the picture is not good enough.

For example, you may decide to bleach your face simply because the mirror showed you some spots and pimples. The mirror will show you exactly how your nails look like, but it would also advise you to put on artificial nails and make your fingers look like claws.

A LOUD VOICE

The voice of your mirror would not stop there, it would let you turn on your television, in order to learn new worldly styles and patterns. It would tell you to compare what you see on the television with what the mirror portrayed as your real appearance.

Another voice that can be compared with the mirror is the voice of the media. Most newspapers and magazines have come up with fashion and style   to tell us that we need to copy the latest fashions. Such paper give us unsolicited updates concerning latest trends. From time to time, they suggest trends which people should adopt in order to keep up with latest styles.

The T.V is so subtle. Often times, it shows seductive clips, in a bid to promote certain body creams and soap. The details may keep you glued to your seat, showing you fascinating styles just to attract your attention. The T.V can be so powerful such that you may watch and sleep off forgetting to turn it off. You must overcome such a powerful negative voice. T.V has been described as an instrument of witchcraft. It is wide and wild in the spread of negative influence. Yeh, this spread looks unstoppable as it continues to spread like wild fire all over the world.

NOTES:

_____

_____

_____

_____

_____

_____

_____

_____

_____

_____

_____

_____

_____

_____

_____

_____

_____

_____

_____

_____

_____

_____

_____

Chapter 19

POWER OVER SATANIC ENTICEMENT

Another voice which we need to contend with is the voice of our parents. We keep hearing their voices day in day out. When their voices become overpowering we have no option than to keep to what they say to us. We often make the mistake of listening to our parents not knowing that our parents may be busy parading worldly wisdom. The voice of your father or mother may compel you to go out of the will of God as a result of their influence over you.

PARENTAL INFLUENCE

Ordinarily; what your parents say about your goals in life may continue to chase shadows in the name of following a pattern that has been adopted for you by your parents

When you listen to your parent's words, such words would stick to your memory. You may remain restless until you have carried out the instructions given to you. We have to move away from the realm of parental opinion. If you linger in that place, you maybe blindfolded and begin to sheepishly follow what your parents say:

Our parents are so near us that their influence cannot be underestimated. We need the power of the Holy Spirit if we must avoid negative influence. Unless we manage negative voices, they may over power us. If you do not control how people try to influence you, you may fall into the pit. You need the power of the word also

> *Let not sin therefore reign in your mortal body, that ye should obey it in the lusts thereof. Neither yields ye your members as instruments of unrighteousness unto sin: but yield yourselves unto God, as those that are alive from the dead, and your members as instruments of righteousness unto God.*
> **Romans 6:12-13**

EVIL MAGNETS

Strange voices operate like magnets as they easily stick. The Bible has cautioned us against worldly or demonic enticements,

> *My son, hears the instruction of thy father, and forsakes not the law of thy mother: For they shall be an ornament of grace unto thy head, and chains about thy neck. My son, if sinners entice thee, consent thou not. If they say, come with us,*

let us lay wait for blood, let us lurk privily for the innocent without cause: Let us swallow them up alive as the grave; and whole, as those that go down into the pit: We shall find all precious substance, we shall fill our houses with spoil: Cast in thy lot among us; let us all have one purse: My son, walk not thou in the way with them; refrain thy foot from their path: For their feet run to evil, and make haste to shed blood. Surely in vain the net is spread in the sight of any bird.
Proverbs 1:8 -17

Sinners are all over the place trying to entice. Enticement can come from friends, neighbours and colleagues. The Bible makes it clear that, enticements will come. But, God's instruction is clear; Consent thou not" God has given us insights into the type of word they would speak

If they say; Come with us, let us lay wait for blood, let us lurk privily for the innocent without cause: **Prov.1:11**

They would speak enticing words

And my speech and my preaching was not with enticing words of man's wisdom, but in demonstration of the Spirit and of power: **1 Corinthians 2:4**

And this I say lest any man should beguile you with enticing words. **Colossians 2:4**

It is unfortunate that those who entice general speak to us more than those who lead us to the path of righteousness. When you listen very often to enticing words, you may not know when you begin to dance to the tune of negative voices. According to the passage, people who speak enticing words would not give up until you listen to them.

THE CHARACTERISTICS

Enticements have the following characteristics.
1.   They are subtle
2.   They are friendly
3.   They are systematic
4.   They are persuasive
5.   They are smooth talkers
6.   They give you points concerning what you stand to gain, if you listen to their voices"

7. Even when you are not easily persuaded, don't give up as they would try another day
8. They show you only one side of the coin, by showing the blind spot.

SATANIC SUBTLETY

Do you know that your friend who gave you a good advice yesterday can become an agent of enticement tomorrow? Parents who took care of you today may be, inadvertently used by the devil tomorrow.

Voices are legion. Voices are compelling. They are subtle. Unfortunately, negative voices have polluted everywhere. You can hardly go through an hour without hearing negative voices.

Negative voices are loud. Voices of enticement are many:. The devil does not give up. He keeps on cajoling, convincing, and persuading those who listen to consider options that are contrary to the plans and purposes of God. Many people have lost the battle to strange voices. A lot of people have been influenced to follow the path of unrighteousness.

COMMON VOICES

Those who are used by the Devil to spread strange voices are sincerely meticulous. They take one step here and another there. They remain persevering until their evil goals are achieved. Negative voices are so terrible that, we must restrain them. Negative voices are so dangerous that we must stop them from spreading further.

Voices of negativity are so common that, we must not allow them to gather any momentum and destroy us. Satanic voices are so loud and we must avoid them. Voices of darkness are so evil, that we must watch our lives lest they penetrate.

We must make use of every godly weapon in order to completely deal with negative voices. It is important that we kill the poison deposited by negatives voices in our lives. We must convert our lives to fire so that negative voices will not have any landing spot. The following steps must be taken in order to deal with negative voices.

IMPORTANT STEPS

The following are the steps you must take in order to overpower negative strange voices.

1. **Recognise, identify and discern negative voices**. There are various types of negative voices. These voices have wicked missions.

Their evil mission is to accomplish the following:

1. They waste destinies
2. They overpower their victims in order to affect them negatively
3. They turn their lives upside down.
4. The mission of the power of the emptier is to empty and remove good things from the people.
5. They destroy
6. They lead their victims astray
7. They lead their victims into confusion
8. They strip their victims naked.
9. They rubbish destinies
10. They chase people away form the place of their blessings
11. They employ the power of household witchcraft to oppress victims.
12. They fight against virtues
13. They re-arrange destinies
14. They antagonise
15. They spread evil rumour
16. They make satanic report to cover-up
17. They steal peace
18. They kill joy
19. They destroy unity
20. They promote division
21. They destroy and defame
22. They produce terrifying fear

23. They paralyse potentials
24. Thy downgrade honour
25. They produce shock
26. They inflict insanity
27. They discourage helpers
28. They spoil relationship
29. They cause chronic distraction
30. They make people to fall into error and do stupid things
31. They promote chronic ignorance

The Bible says that, by their fruit we shall know them. When you notice the symptoms above in your life, then you should know that the enemy is at work.

2. **You must be filled with the Holy Spirit**. The only panacea for dealing with negative voices is to be filled with the Holy Spirit. When you are spirit filled, you will spot negative voices a far off. Even if the enemy tries to disguise, you will know that there is an agenda of darkness to lead you into captivity through evil voices. When you are filled with the Holy Spirit, you will know when God speaks and when the devil speaks.

    You have to fill yourself with the Holy Spirit. This will demand fasting and aggressive prayers. When you are baptised with the Holy Ghost, you must move ahead and become filled and drunken with Holy Spirit. Without the power of the Holy Spirit you cannot say no to evil or negative voices. It is embarrassing, for a believer to respond to an evil voice and follow the instruction of darkness. This can only happen when lives are shallow

A brother was openly embarrassed, because his spiritual level was too low He lacked the power of the Holy Spirit which would have made him reject an evil voice.

He was simply reading in the Library preparing for an important examination. All of a sudden, something happened to him, people came around and found out that he had slept off. That is not the end of the story they found him deeply asleep with his trousers wet and urine on the floor. They had to tap him in order to wake him up.

The brother was embarrassed. He narrated how he started sleeping, he lamented saying; "I am in trouble. So, that lady finally caught up with me". When asked what he meant, he told the story of a lady he just met.

He narrated how he started urinating in the dream at the sound of the voice of the lady. He just could not resist the urge to pass urine compulsively He was highly embarrassed. He had to go for deliverance.

After the deliverance session, he prayed for the baptism of the Holy Spirit. Since then he has learnt his lesson.

3. **Issue a letter of divorce.** You must sack the voice, lest they lead you astray
4. **Put on the righteousness of God.** Barricade your life with the power of the Holy Spirit, with that kind of power, you will be able to overpower all the powers of darkness.

> *For the Son of man is come to seek and to save that which was lost.*
> **Luke 19:10**

5. Load your life with practical Bible study
6. Load your Spirit with melody of God's songs.
7. Pray to be hot spiritually
8   Check out on who you move together i.e. your friend, your friend either add to you or subtract from you
9. Don't stand against truth in any form and please run from negative fellows.

PUBLICATIONS BY DR. D. K. OLUKOYA

1. Be Prepared
2. Bewitchment Must Die
3. Biblical Principles of Dream Interpretation
4. Born Great, but Tied Down
5. Breakthrough Prayers For Business Professional
6. Brokenness
7. Can God?
8. Can God Trust You?
9. Criminals In The House Of God
10. Command The Morning
11. Contending For The Kingdom
12. Dealing With Local Satanic Technology
13. Dealing With Witchcraft Barbers
14. Dealing With Hidden Curses
15. Dealing With Satanic Exchange
16. Dealing With The Evil Powers Of Your Father's House
17. Dealing With Unprofitable Roots
18. Deliverance: God's Medicine Bottle
19. Deliverance By Fire '
2U. Deliverance From Limiting Powers
21. Deliverance From Spirit Husband And Spirit Wife
22. Deliverance Of The Conscience
23. Deliverance Of The Head
24. Destiny Clinic

25. Disgracing Soul Hunters
26. Destroying The Evil Umbrella
27. Drawers of Power From The Heavenlies
28. Dominion Prosperity
29. Evil Appetite
30. Evil Umbrella
31. Facing Both Ways
32. Family Deliverance
33.. Failure In The School Of Prayer
34. Freedom From The Grip Of Witchcraft
35. From Adversity To Testimony.
36. For We Wrestle...
37. Holy Cry
38. Holy Fever
39. Holiness Unto The Lord
40. How To Obtain Personal Deliverance (Second Edition)
41. How To Pray When Surrounded By The Enemies
42. Idols Of The Heart
43. Is This What They Died For?
44. Limiting God
45. Madness Of The Heart
46. H\Meat For Champions
47. Medicine For Winners
48. Open Heavens Through Holy Disturbance
49. Overpowering Witchcraft
50. Paying The Evil Tithes

OTHER BOOKS AUTHORED BY SISTER SHADE OLUKOYA

1. Power To Fulfill Your Destiny
2. Principles Of A Successful Marriage
3. The Call Of God
4. The Daughters Of Philip
5. When Your Destiny Is Under Attack
6. Woman of Wonders

www.ingramcontent.com/pod-product-compliance
Lightning Source LLC
Chambersburg PA
CBHW071437090426
42737CB00011B/1682